Josette Baer

Saul Goodman—the American Candide?
Essays on Politics, Philosophy and Film

With a foreword by Wolfgang Rother

Josette Baer

SAUL GOODMAN— THE AMERICAN CANDIDE?

Essays on Politics, Philosophy and Film

With a foreword by Wolfgang Rother

Bibliografische Information der Deutschen Nationalbibliothek
Die Deutsche Nationalbibliothek verzeichnet diese Publikation in der Deutschen Nationalbibliografie; detaillierte bibliografische Daten sind im Internet über http://dnb.d-nb.de abrufbar.

Bibliographic information published by the Deutsche Nationalbibliothek
Die Deutsche Nationalbibliothek lists this publication in the Deutsche Nationalbibliografie; detailed bibliographic data are available in the Internet at http://dnb.d-nb.de.

ISBN-13: 978-3-8382-1674-4
© *ibidem*-Verlag, Hannover • Stuttgart 2024
Alle Rechte vorbehalten

Das Werk einschließlich aller seiner Teile ist urheberrechtlich geschützt. Jede Verwertung außerhalb der engen Grenzen des Urheberrechtsgesetzes ist ohne Zustimmung des Verlages unzulässig und strafbar. Dies gilt insbesondere für Vervielfältigungen, Übersetzungen, Mikroverfilmungen und elektronische Speicherformen sowie die Einspeicherung und Verarbeitung in elektronischen Systemen.

All rights reserved. No part of this publication may be reproduced, stored in or introduced into a retrieval system, or transmitted, in any form, or by any means (electronic, mechanical, photocopying, recording or otherwise) without the prior written permission of the publisher. Any person who does any unauthorized act in relation to this publication may be liable to criminal prosecution and civil claims for damages.

Printed in the EU

DEDICATED TO

H. G. TUDOR

Table of Contents

Acknowledgements 9

Introduction and Method 11

Foreword by Wolfgang Rother, University of Zurich UZH .. 13

I. Thomas Sowell's *Black Rednecks and White Liberals*: *The Best of Enemies* 21

II. Simone de Beauvoir's Girl: *La Journée de la Jupe (Skirt Day)* 37

III. Immanuel Kant's Perpetual War: *Fauda* 55

IV. Antique Concepts of Love and Hatred: *The Lost Daughter* 113

V. Niccolò Machiavelli and the CIA: *Homeland* 151

VI. Thomas Hobbes in New Mexico: *Breaking Bad* 197

VII. Voltaire's *Candide* or Optimism: *Better Call Saul* 237

Appendix

Index 263

Acknowledgements

Wolfgang Rother, the author of the foreword, has been my friend and colleague at the Department of Philosophy at UZH for many years. He is the editor of CONEXUS, the online journal of senior scholars at UZH. Thanks to his philosophical curiosity and editorial generosity, I began to write about aspects of political theory in film—and this book is the result.

Peter Horváth, Jaroslav Mihálik and Martin Švikruha are great bosses—they are making my employment at UCM Trnava a sheer joy. Tatiana Tökölyová and my colleagues at the UCM Faculty of Social Sciences are like family to me. I thank Peter Thomas Hill, who has been teaching me scholarly English. One never ceases to learn.

Note that the essays about *Breaking Bad*, *Homeland*, and *The Lost Daughter* have been previously published in CONEXUS, and I thank Wolfgang Rother and CONEXUS for their permission to publish them here. Note also that in the essays about *Breaking Bad*, *Better Call Saul*, *Homeland* and *Fauda* I have indicated the series and episodes without time stamps. I have used time stamps only in the essays about the films *The Lost Daughter*, *La Journée de la Jupe* (*Skirt Day*) and *The Best of Enemies*.

I hope that the reader who likes film shall enjoy this little book. Needless to say, but I am saying it anyway: all errors and mistakes are mine.

Josette Baer
Trnava, Zurich and Prague
February 2024

Introduction and Method

This little book is meant for readers who like film. Naturally, I cannot prove that the screenwriters were inspired by theoretical considerations, but that is not my point. I want to draw the readers' attention to the way principles, ideas and thinking about political theory can explain a film script and its main statement or message. My analysis of film plots is intended to widen our horizons and also deepen our understanding of cinema's take on these complex questions.

If we accept a simple definition of film as storytelling with optical means, then that story we see unfolding on the screen operates like a written story: after the introduction of the *personae*, the plot presents the film's main theme with several subplots. Films usually end with a happy or unhappy end, thus revealing the plot as a comedy or tragedy. My method is interdisciplinary, thus very simple: I look at the film and interpret the plot with aspects of political theory, which I have identified in the story. The readers will have to decide for themselves if my arguments and analysis are convincing.

Wolfgang Rother

Why we should not consider films as products of mass culture but as narratives whose philosophical core needs to be uncovered

Violence and hatred, crime and war have characterised human civilisation since the beginning. Murder and manslaughter from the very beginning. According to the biblical myth, Cain kills his brother Abel for base motives. Why is this so? This is a question that still puzzles people today, not only philosophers and theologians, but especially the latter. Social and political reality, especially in our day and age, stands in the starkest possible contrast to the existence of a wise and benevolent Creator and a world ordered according to principles of reason and justice. *Si Deus est, unde malum?* If God exists, where does evil come from? Even if the answer that Leibniz developed in 1710 in his *Essais de Théodicée sur la Bonté de Dieu, la Liberté de l'Homme et l'Origine du Mal* (Theodicy: Essays of on the Goodness of God, the Freedom of Man and the Origin of Evil)—evil is the price that people pay for their freedom—is not without good theological and philosophical arguments, the theological and philosophical arguments he makes for his theodicy are based on his optimism that we live in the best of all possible worlds; that God, in his wisdom, his goodness and his love for mankind, had no choice but to create the world as it is. An echo of this view can still be found in Hegel's famous and notorious dictum in the *Elements of the Philosophy of Right* of 1821: "What is reasonable is real; and what is real is reasonable."

Hegel can be accused of opportunism and Leibniz of a large dose of naivety. Voltaire already did the latter in 1759 in his *Candide ou l'Optimisme—candidus*, the white man with a clean slate; the pure and innocent man who not only experiences the horrors of war but also becomes a murderer himself. It is obvious to think of Saul Goodman from the television series *Better Call Saul* as Voltaire's Candide, as the title of this book suggests. Voltaire's satire paints the picture of an optimist as a political-philosophical archetype, which is also represented by the film hero Saul Goodman, whose *nomen* is *omen* (Saul before the Damascus experience and the good man) and whose homophone "S'all Good, Man" (this is the advertising slogan of Goodman's company) casually sums up Leibniz's optimism, even if Goodman—the contradiction to the best of all possible worlds could not be more blatant—is a felon who is sentenced to sixty-eight years in prison (Essay VII).

The essays collected here under the title of the "American Candide", whose cover depicts the sage head of the French Enlightenment philosopher and critic Voltaire, are subtitled "Philosophy and Film". But how do philosophy and film go together? For the founders of critical theory, Max Horkheimer and Theodor W. Adorno, not at all. In their *Dialectic of Enlightenment*, which was written in exile in California, especially in the long and central chapter on the culture industry, films, as they were produced in the nearby dream factory Hollywood, figure as the epitome of shallow mass culture and aesthetic barbarism, as goods that are consumed and of interest to the producers not from an artistic but solely from an economic point of view.

However, in my view, this is no reason at all not to deal with the products of the culture industry from a philosophical perspective. It is by no means a question of wanting to ascribe philosophical dignity to films, of ennobling them as an object of philosophical reflection and investigation. What justifies the philosophical preoccupation with phenomena of popular culture? They are, to take up a phrase from Hegel's *Phenomenology of Spirit* from 1807, figures of the spirit, that is, not only figures of consciousness, but also figures of the concrete world and its history. Manifested in films—even if one can argue about their aesthetic quality and their quality as products of mass culture—there is what appears important to the people of a certain cultural sphere in a certain epoch. And these are the great, ultimately existential, philosophical themes that concern them. What films perhaps have in common with philosophy is that they are, to again invoke Hegel's *Elements of the Philosophy of Right*, their time captured in thought.

Whether the films and scriptwriters are aware of this, whether they can or could present the thematised figures of consciousness in adequate philosophical language, is irrelevant. Because a film is above all a narrative, a story. In Greek terms, it is a myth with an inherent logos, a rational, philosophical core that needs to be uncovered. The close relationship between myth and philosophy was already thematised by Aristotle in his *Metaphysics*. According to Aristotle, the friend of myth, φιλόμυθος (*philomythos*), is also a friend of wisdom, φιλόσοφος (*philosophos*). The philosophical core is already contained in the pre-conceptual myth, as well as in the narrative of a film. The film narrative always points beyond its own sphere of the particular, individual and paradigmatic into the sphere of the universal and philosophical. It is—to quote Hegel one last time, this time his *Lectures on the History of Philosophy* in the Heidelberg transcript of 1817—like the myth a "work of fantasising reason"; "the thinking mind, however, must seek out the substantial content, the thought, the philosophical that is implicit in it". It is precisely this, namely to seek out, find and make explicit what is implicitly contained in the film, that the present essays aspire to and fulfil in an exemplary manner.

The critical perspective that films are mass products of the culture industry and that the film industry is primarily interested in making big money ignores the fact that films, at least those dealt with in this book, address relevant existential, philosophical, political, and social issues. After all, who would deny that the problem of racial discrimination dealt with in Robert Bissell's *The Best of Enemies* is a politically and socially explosive issue? (Essay I) Even if one considers the happy ending, the reconciliation of the black activist with the white Ku Klux Klan leader, to be too unrealistic and harmonising—which it is not, because the film is based on a true story: *The Best of Enemies* shows a perspective, shows how hatred can and will be overcome through friendship.

The story of Jean-Paul Lilienfeld's *La Journée de la Jupe* (*Skirt Day*) is just as relevant from a cultural and socio-philosophical perspective as it is from a feminist one (Essay II). How does a country that was the scene of a world-historical revolution in the name of freedom, equality, and secularism in 1789 and that produced the founder of modern feminism, Simone de Beauvoir, deal with the sexist culture in the violent Arab banlieues today? No happy ending this time: The protagonist, the teacher Sonia Bergerac, who always wears a skirt as a sign of female self-empowerment and therefore attracts the wrath and contempt of the Arab youths, takes her class hostage and dies from a gunshot.

Another sadly topical issue is the award-winning Israeli television series *Fauda*, which focuses on the ongoing Israeli-Palestinian conflict and the fight of an Israeli special unit against the terror of Hamas and Hezbollah (Essay III). As a philosopher socialised in the German-speaking world, it is only natural for her to discuss the ideas from Kant's 1795 treatise *On Perpetual Peace*. Isn't eternal peace rather utopian and political reality eternal war, as the title of the corresponding essay by Josette Baer states?

Maggie Gyllenhaal's film *The Lost Daughter*, which is about a university professor who has two children whom she leaves for a love affair but returns to after three years, can be analysed with a view to the major theme of love and hate (Essay IV). The philosophical background to the analysis, which concludes by discussing the question raised by anti-natalism as to whether we should have children or not, is provided by Hannah Arendt's 1929 dissertation, *Love and Saint Augustine*, and Plutarch's comments on hatred in his *Moralia*.

It is also illuminating how the CIA agent Carrie Mathison, the heroine of the thriller *Homeland*, is read as a figure in whom three important principles of Niccolò Machiavelli's political theory are united: firstly, prudence and humanity, secondly, the need to appear as a person with good qualities, and thirdly, to behave in politics in such a way that one is not hated (Essay V).

What is finally negotiated in the popular and successful television series *Breaking Bad*, with its protagonist, the polite chemistry teacher Walter White, who turns into a criminal in Albuquerque's drug underworld in order to secure his family's financial existence, are central concepts of political philosophy: Thomas Hobbes' theory of the war of all against all and his social anthropology of man as the wolf of man as well as Hannah Arendt's theory of power and violence (Essay VI).

Why this book is important: It is by no means merely a matter of giving a philosophically guided interpretation of films and integrating philosophical aspects into their interpretation, but above all it is about an interdisciplinary cooperation that does justice to the films and their philosophical core, a cooperation between philosophy and art—and film is an art form par excellence, a multimedia work of art that presents stories in texts, drama, images, and music. Philosophy and art can and should complement each other dialectically, to pick up on a thought from Adorno's *Aesthetic Theory*, published in 1970 from his estate. They are dependent on each other: art on philosophy, which exposes its core in order to say what art cannot say; and philosophy on art, because it presents what philosophy itself cannot say.

This important book represents a successful attempt to bring philosophy and film into dialogue with each other in this way.

Gebenstorf, February 2024

I. Thomas Sowell's *Black Rednecks and White Liberals*: *The Best of Enemies*

Introduction

Thomas Sowell's (*1930) essay "Black Rednecks and White Liberals"[1] explains the history of slavery in the USA and its connection with the contemporary so-called black ghetto culture. His text is superbly researched; his analysis of the often ruthless and violent behaviour of some black citizens and communities can be traced back to the years of slavery, when white Americans in the South often treated their black slaves worse than cattle.

Indeed, one is astonished to learn that the behaviour of the whites has its origins in the immigrant communities from the Celtic fringe, Scotland, and Ireland. Immigrants of these communities had settled in the south of what would become the USA in the centuries prior to slavery—and, back home on the British Isles, they were being civilized by the British, who, in the 18th and 19th centuries, were integrating these regions and people to English culture:

> "More is involved here than a mere parallel between blacks and Southern whites. What is involved is a common subculture that goes back for centuries, which has encompassed everything from ways of talking to attitudes toward education, violence and sex—and

---

[1] Thomas Sowell, "Black Rednecks and White Liberals", in *Black Rednecks and White Liberals* (New York: Encounter Books, 2006), 1-63.

which originated not in the South, but in those parts of the British Isles from which white Southerners came."[2]

Traits of such behaviour can manifest themselves in some black communities, certainly not in all. What one can learn from Sowell's analysis is that contemporary simplistic accusations of racism argue with the Southern slavery system of the 19th century, a system the North abolished by winning the Civil War (1861–1865). Today, bad behaviour of blacks is being explained with past white oppression.

Now, how did the white Southerners behave? Sowell identifies the main characteristic features of white redneck culture: pride and violence;[3] poor economic activity or the lack of entrepreneurship;[4] intellectual activity or disregard for education;[5] sexual activity and religion:[6]

> "What the rednecks or crackers brought with them across the ocean was a whole constellation of attitudes, values and behaviour patterns that might have made sense in the world in which they had lived for centuries, but which would prove to be counterproductive in the world to which they were going—and counterproductive to the blacks who would live in their midst for centuries before emerging into freedom and

---

[2] Sowell, 1.
[3] Sowell, 7-13.
[4] Sowell, 13-22.
[5] Sowell, 22-23.
[6] Sowell, 23-27.

migrating to the great urban centers of the United States, taking with them similar values."[7]

What did this behaviour look like? Sowell lists the following, referring to his sources: cultural values and social patterns consisted of an aversion to work; proneness to violence; neglect of or disinterest in education; sexual promiscuity; drunkenness, and reckless searches for excitement.[8] One can identify some of these characteristics in the community of black rednecks, especially in the behaviour and values of members of 'gangsta rap' and its barbarism.[9] Gang violence, a life determined by criminal behaviour, drug and alcohol abuse and the idea that education is for white folks only, seem to be the features of contemporary black identity:

> "The thuggish gutter words and brutal hoodlum lifestyle of 'gangsta rap' musicians are not merely condoned but glorified by many white intellectuals—and 'understood' by others lacking the courage to take responsibility for siding with savages."[10]

Whether we like it or not, Sowell has convincing facts- alcohol and drug abuse, sexual promiscuity, and the disinterest in education prompt bad results: children born of wedlock; teenage pregnancy; families without fathers, that is, no male role models; neglected and lonely male children who join the neighbourhood gang, because the gang has

---

[7] Sowell, 6.
[8] Sowell, 6.
[9] Sowell, 55.
[10] Sowell, 55.

strict rules, thus operating as *Ersatz* family; socialisation into violence by gang rules; lack of personal hygiene, and a painful lack of personal responsibility.

How can I, as a child, learn hygiene, responsibility, and discipline if I wake up every morning in a filthy flat, seeing my parents passed out on some substance? How to improve without role models? Who is to blame for this social misery? To survive, I need help, coping mechanisms—thus, why not join the gang in my neighbourhood? They have rules and provide a home with a catechism of behaviour. That is the rational choice of a neglected child.

Often, black leaders put forward accusations of slavery, blaming white oppression for black failure. Yet, one might find that this issue is a bit more complicated. Patronizing those blacks who do not share their beliefs, the BLM movement[11] claims to represent all blacks in their fight for equality and justice. Yet, BLM fails to explain why musicians such as the band Earth, Wind & Fire, Michael Jackson, Beyoncé, and Diana Ross, to name but a few, are global house-hold names, their songs being played all over the world. Actors such as Sidney Poitier, Denzel Washington, Halle Berry, and Viola Davis have excelled because of their talent and professional acumen. The stellar careers of Simone Biles, Kobe Bryant, Muhammad Ali, and Serena Williams prove that to be successful in sports has nothing to do with the colour of your skin.

Londoner Naomi Campbell was the first black model to grace the prestigious cover of French VOGUE in the 1980s—

---

[11] https://blacklivesmatter.com; accessed 17 December 2023.

and that because white super models Linda Evangelista and Christy Turlington refused to take on modelling jobs as long as VOGUE kept ignoring black Naomi. Turlington and Evangelista thus stood up for their friend Campbell, making the fashion business aware of its anti-black bias. Excelled have, furthermore, journalist Candace Owens, author Shelby Steele, neurosurgeon Ben Carson, and philosophy professor Cornel West, to name but the most prominent.

Is a nation racist who votes half-black Barack Obama[12] US president for two terms? I certainly do not want to diminish the real suffering of black US citizens, but to simplify such a complicated issue with one-sided accusations is not helpful.

Furthermore, Sowell explains most convincingly, how the civil rights movement, embodied by Martin Luther King Jr. (1929–1968) became a moral endeavour and task of white liberals. This engagement of white liberals, speaking for the blacks, and accusing the whites of racism and discrimination of blacks, has been deepening the gap between black and white US citizens. In German, we have a wise slogan: "Das Gegenteil von gut ist nicht böse, aber gut gemeint."[13] It explains that one can have the best intentions but the results of one's activities can prompt a negative outcome, i.e. well-meant but badly exercised, badly done. Sowell on the white liberals' apologetics for the bad behaviour of some black citizens:

---

[12] https://www.whitehouse.gov/about-the-white-house/presidents/barack-obama/; accessed 17 December 2023.

[13] https://german.stackexchange.com/questions/1753/herkunft-der-redewendung-das-gegenteil-von-gut-ist-gut-gemeint; accessed 17 December 2023.

"White liberals long denied that there were higher crime rates among blacks by pointing to the imperfections of crime statistics in general or more specifically, claiming that blacks are simply arrested more often for things that whites would not be arrested for. But if the imperfections of crime statistics were the real problem, then discussions could be limited to murder statistics, since dead bodies are not ignored, whether they are black or white, and neither are murderers, whatever their race. But murder statistics show the same disproportionate number of crimes by blacks as other statistics do. While murder statistics might provide more accuracy, they would not provide white liberals with a means of evading the obvious."[14]

I am no specialist of black US history, but if Sowell is right, and I think that he is, then the promotion and defence of black interests by white liberals seem to me to be of an authoritarian and self-appointed nature. If I am elected to an executive political position, I respect citizens and listen to their grievances, but I do not patronize them. I take them seriously and I should not treat them as inferior just because I think I know better. I might be wrong. From this follows that I should find a pragmatic solution to their grievances, treating them as equal citizens, whatever the colour of their skin. That is why Sowell condemns the affirmative action[15] programs that were well meant but prompted bad results; they are patronizing, indeed, infantilizing the blacks, thus treating

---

[14] Sowell, 53.
[15] Very informative is https://www.aaaed.org/aaaed/History_of_Affirmative_Action.asp; accessed 31 December 2023.

them as inferior citizens. Allegedly, or so white liberals must think, blacks need the help and support of the US government as the righting of the wrongs of slavery:

> "The general orientation of white liberals has been one of 'What can *we* do for *them*?' What blacks can do for themselves has not only been of lesser interest, much of what blacks have in fact already done for themselves has been overshadowed by liberal attempts to get them special dispensation—whether affirmative action reparations for slavery or other race-based benefits—even when the net effect of these dispensations has been much less than the effects of blacks own self-advancement." [16]

In the years following the murder of MLK, the South was violating the constitution by discriminating blacks. In those dark years, black citizens, supported by white citizens who were not afraid to stand up against the strong ku klux klan (kkk),[17] had to fight for their constitutionally granted rights.

What Hannah Arendt (1906–1973) meant with her famous saying "the right to have rights"[18] focuses on the legal status of refugees and displaced persons after WWII. She questioned the moral and legal validity of inalienable human rights. Her thoughts do not apply to our case, to the blacks in the US South, because they already had these rights granted

---

[16] Sowell, 55.
[17] A fascinating insight into the terrorist group is https://www.fbi.gov/history/famous-cases/kkk-series; accessed 17 December 2023.
[18] An interesting summary on https://criticallegalthinking.com/2019/07/12/hannah-arendt-right-to-have-rights/accessed 17 December 2023.

by the constitution. Yet, in North Carolina in the 1970s, the constitutional reality black citizens were experiencing every day had nothing in common with the stipulations of the US constitution. There was a huge gap between constitutional reality and constitutional text.

If I happen to be born black, and US citizenship grants my civil rights, there can be no exceptions nor excuses for me not to enjoy the same rights as everybody else, regardless of the colour of my skin, sexual orientation, and religious and political beliefs. A right that exists only on paper and is not being realized, is no right at all; it is an idea, expressed in beautiful, yet shallow words. But a right that is enshrined in and protected by the constitution, a right that I can claim, not just today or tomorrow and not just for me, but also for my children and grandchildren, always and forever, is a real right.

The Best of Enemies

> "Because all our blood is the same colour when it comes out—I haven't seen any blood different yet than the colour of mine."[19]

Let us now have a look at history; let us delve into bad times. Thanks to the individual courage and responsibility exercised by both black and white citizens, the lives of Southern blacks

---

[19] 1:44. The film lasts 2 hours and 13 minutes. The minutes I refer to are counted from the beginning of the film, thus Ann's quote is 1 minute and 44 seconds into the film.

turned to the better. This film[20] about the history of the US civil rights movement is unforgettable. Its message is strong. *The Best of Enemies* shows how the race-based hostility between black activist Ann Atwater (1935–2016) and ku klux klan leader Claiborne Paul Ellis (1927–2005), aka C. P., develops into a friendship, and how C. P. is increasingly questioning his beliefs once he is confronted with courageous Atwater. Atwater is portrayed by Taraji P. Henson, and Sam Rockwell plays the klan leader to perfection. Both main actors' performance and the screen writing are superb, and I expected the film to be, at least, nominated for an Oscar. No such luck.

The plot is based on a true story,[21] demonstrating that hatred can turn into respect and friendship, that people can live peacefully side by side once they have overcome beliefs that are grounded in hatred, contempt, and violence. Once I understand that the other is also a human being, we have more in common than what the powers that be are preaching. Enmity and hostility, violence, and hatred are festering in situations when people are not educated enough to see through political manipulation, relying on the preaching of leaders who pursue their vested self-interest. Critical thinking requires education, the capability of thinking things through independently. Sometimes, however, people are just evil.

---

[20] https://www.imdb.com/title/tt4807408/; accessed 10 December 2023.
[21] https://www.amazon.com/Best-Enemies-Race-Redemption-South/dp/0807858692; accessed 17 December 2023.

Durham, North Carolina, in the summer of 1971: Black citizens, led by Ann Atwater, demonstrate in front of the mayor's office against the miserable living conditions in the apartments they rent from local property owner Greenfield. Ann and a young black women have a meeting with the mayor, explaining the problems of the black tenants. The mayor grants Ann a time slot to speak at the next meeting of the city council. In the meantime, Ellis, the owner of a garage and gas station, speaks at a klan meeting and then listens to teenager Leonard one of the young members has recruited. Asked by Ellis why he wants to join, the teenager replies that he wants to protect the white race in America from the communist niggers and the Jews. Leonard has learnt the klan's credo well, and Ellis shows him the membership card: "You see that? One day, this will be your most prized possession. And it will give you everything you need in your life: brotherhood, standing in the community and a sense of pride that you're part of something bigger than yourself. [...] But most importantly, it will be a reminder every day that you'll no longer be an outsider."[22] Leonard is now a member of the klan's youth corps. The klan honours loyalty, the hatred of everybody who does not heed its creed, and promotes an unrepenting propensity to violence and the belief that women are inferior, at the service of men.

Three drunk klan members, all male and in their early thirties, engage in terrorizing citizens whom they believe are committing crimes against the white race. They wait in their car in front of a house, where a young woman lives. Allegedly,

---

[22] 7:02; 7:03.

she has a black boyfriend. Once the woman is in her house, back home from work, they shoot at the house, destroying furniture. This is not only psychological terror, but also physical terror. Why? By shooting at the house, knowing that she is there, they are deliberately taking into account that one of the many bullets they are firing might kill her. That would be murder—the deliberate killing of a human being for racial reasons. The young woman survives, but she will have to redecorate. Durham City Council won't pay for the redecoration. Where is the evidence that it was the klan that destroyed her home? If the young woman took this case to court, it would be word against word. She has no evidence, no eyewitnesses.

Ann is preparing her speech for the city council and has collected seventy-nine signatures and complaints; the black citizens are accusing Greenfield of code violation, and the housing commission, all white, elder males, grants Greenfield's lawyer ninety days to improve the living conditions in his properties.

Ellis has lunch with his family. Wife Mary, portrayed by Anne Heche (1969–2022), is a clever and loyal woman. She does not speak much, but when she raises her voice, she makes sense. She reproaches her husband that they are in a dire financial situation—he should consider selling gas also to the blacks. Mary and C. P. have four children, and Ellis' love for his handicapped son who has trisomy-21 and lives in a psychiatric clinic is most touching. He visits him often and feeds him, spending time with him. Klan leader and racist C. P. is no adherent of Nazi euthanasia; his belief in white supremacy has limits. These intellectual limits shall be crucial for his complete change of mind later.

We have seen Ann and C. P., the two main characters, acting in their communities—and one has to admire the accuracy of Sowell's analysis: the white klan members engage in heavy drinking and always look dishevelled and unhygienic, sporting sweat-stained shirts, greasy hair, dirty nails and yellow teeth. They regularly meet at a shooting range, asserting their virility, using foul language. They are not only racist but also sexist, and their vile antisemitism is most primitive, based on Hitler's *Mein Kampf*. In their way of thinking, women are second class citizens, born to be at the service of men, while blacks are no humans at all. Jews are anti-Christs who are conspiring to rule the world, financially enslaving the white race in America.

The black citizens, on the other hand, are impeccably turned out, wear ironed shirts, trousers, and skirts, have clean hair, skin and nails and are anxious and alert because of what they are experiencing on a daily basis: to be treated as inferior, to have to make way on the pavement when a white person is approaching. They care about hygiene because they do not want to be called dirty and the n-word. They always look freshly washed. Clearly, the black parents teach their children discipline and hygiene. They also have a strong sense of community: they stick together and support each other, because they have learnt that even judges can be corrupted. In their way of thinking, the greatness of the US constitution applies only to white folks.

While Ann's two girls are at school, the smoke alarm goes off, and the children are being evacuated. Nobody has died, but the half-burnt East End Elementary school is no longer operational. The black community asks the city council to move the children to the white school, Durham Elementary, so they can finish the school year. The council announces that such decision is subject to a vote. Naturally, the white citizens protest against the charrette, suggested by a member of the NAACP (National Association for the Advancement of Colored People).[23]

A charrette is a public meeting or workshop that pursues a distinct goal or aims at solving a problem of society or a community. Bill Riddick from Raleigh, NC, arrives in Durham to organize a charrette to solve the school problem. He invites Ann and C. P. to act as co-chairs and representatives of the divided communities. The charrette's goal is the integration of all children, black and white, into one school. Planned are ten meetings. Once both have agreed—Ellis needs some persuasion from Bill—a local newspaper announces the upcoming first charrette meeting with the title "Klan member and Negro activist".

At the first meeting, the black pastor suggests that each party should make a wish how to end the charrette in the evenings; he announces the singing of gospel music that represents the Christian spirit of the black citizens. Ellis announces the wish of the whites: to display klan literature, insignia, and the Confederate flag to explain to the blacks why the white race is superior. After a heated dispute with Ann, Ellis goes to his car and gets out his shotgun. Obviously, he wants to intimidate Ann and Bill. Ann provokes him, asking

---

[23] https://naacp.org; accessed 13 December 2023.

if he knows the bible at all. Of course, I have read the bible, C. P. replies, and adds that he even goes to church on Sundays. Feisty Ann leaves him speechless: "Well, then you ought to know, C. P." "Know what?" "Same god made you, made me."[24]

The daily charrette meetings are slowly bringing together blacks and whites. A clever method: the procedure of daily meetings, talking to each other, having lunch together and getting to know the others is de-escalating the racial divide, and, at the same time, diminishing the klan's hold over the whites. Now, blacks and whites are talking to each other. The charrette's goal is exactly that—a beginning. They do not have to like each other, but they get to know each other on a personal basis. White Betty meets black Lucy; black Tom talks to white Jim.

When Ann learns about Ellis' handicapped son Larry, her sense of humanity sets a way of thinking into motion that will end C. P.'s loyalty to the klan for good. With the help of an acquaintance, a black nurse, Ann makes sure that Larry can stay alone in his room; after the hospital had moved another boy into the room, Larry was deeply upset.

We see C. P. slowly questioning his beliefs. At a baseball game, he walks over to chat with local grocery shop owner Lee Tromblay. He brings him a beer. Tromblay is shunned by the whites because he has several black employees. Ellis asks him why he employs blacks, and Tromblay replies that his deputy manager is the best person he has ever met. They had

---

[24] 52:00.

been to Vietnam together, on two tours, and the black man had saved his life.

In the meantime, wife Mary visits Ann to thank her for her help with Larry. The women get along very well. We can see how corrupt the community's council is when two police officers show up at Tromblay's shop: there is a security issue with his fire alarm, and Lee needs to shut down the shop. This puts him under financial pressure; his livelihood is threatened. Ellis receives a honourable medal at a klan meeting, and one can see his feelings on his face—he is not happy. There is something going on in his mind. Doubts about the rightfulness of the klan's beliefs are festering in C. P.'s mind.

After the ten charrette meetings, the day of voting has come. The senate members, six white and six black citizens, represent their communities. The vote addresses the crucial issue: school integration, to have black and white children being taught together in one school. This would mean the end of segregation in educational terms.

The voting procedure is mind-boggling, the atmosphere tense. When C. P. is asked to cast his vote, we see him standing at the speaker's dais, silent, thinking. This is a moment not only of excellent screen writing but also of superb acting: Sam Rockwell is a most accomplished actor, impersonating C. P. and his change of mind. His kkk buddies, sure that they can rely on him to vote no, are expectingly grinning at him. Then—the shock, not only for the whites, but also for the blacks: C. P. tears apart his kkk membership card and says "So, my problem is, I don't have any need for this anymore."[25] He votes in favour of school integration.

After Ellis' vote, his former kkk buddies set fire to his business, trying to intimidate him. When Bill leaves town to return home to Raleigh, he makes sure that Durham's black citizens line up to buy gas at C. P.'s station to express their gratitude, since his vote was the crucial last one. C. P. Ellis turned from a believing klan leader to an advocate of equality, realizing the US constitution in Durham, NC. Ann and he, touring the South to inform people about civil rights, were friends until they died.

Conclusion

What can we learn from Thomas Sowell? Rational thinking and a superb understanding of the facts of the US race issue, especially after the BLM riots. Also, we learn from him that education, discipline, and tolerance are vital human values.

MLK had a convincing message, hoping for justice and equality that is based on character, not on the colour of one's skin. To me, Thomas Sowell is not only an accomplished academic, but also a person who embodies the principal values of the Enlightenment: reason, rationality, matter of factness, and tolerance. Perhaps the most important message of his essay and the film *The Best of Enemies* is know-how, the know-how how to deal with the racism issue, not only in the US, but everywhere.

---

[25] 1:55:32.

II. Simone de Beauvoir's Girl:
La Journée de la Jupe (Skirt Day)[1]

This essay is dedicated to all kind and selfless teachers, wherever they live, whatever conditions they have to put up with—you are heroes, not just for one day!
Thank you, David Bowie

> "Sonia Bergerac teaches French at a 'difficult' high school.
> Sonia Bergerac wears skirt although the principal advises her against.
> [...]
> Sonia Bergerac is afraid.
> Sonia Bergerac takes anti-depressants.
> Sonia Bergerac finds a weapon in the bag of a student.
> Sonia Bergerac has just taken her entire class hostage."[2]

---

[1] https://www.imdb.com/title/tt1286809/; accessed 28 January 2024.
[2] The original French text on the back cover of the DVD *La Journée de la Jupe*: "Sonia Bergerac est prof de français dans un college 'difficile'. Sonia Bergerac vient en jupe bien que le proviseur le lui déconseille. [...] Sonia Bergerac a peur. Sonia Bergerac prend des antidépresseurs. Sonia Bergerac a trouvé une arme dans le sac de l'un de ses élèves. Sonia Bergerac vient de prendre sa classe en otage ..."
The last name 'Bergerac' could be an inter-textual hint, referring the viewer to the drama *Cyrano de Bergerac* (1897) by Edmond Rostand, on https://www.britannica.com/topic/Cyrano-de-Bergerac-play-by-Rostand; accessed 23 February 2024. The drama's most beautiful interpretation is the 1990 film by Jean-Paul Rappeneau with Gérard Départdieu as Cyrano and Anne Brochet as Roxane; see https://www.imdb.com/title/tt0099334/; accessed 23 February 2024. Cyrano, an aristocrat from south-western Aquitaine, loves elegant and

Simone de Beauvoir (1908–1986) was a French philosopher and feminist; her famous study *The Second Sex*[3] explains how, after WWII, women became a socio-economic factor in Western societies, what problems they faced in their relationships with parents, fiancés, and husbands and in their lives as professionals in the workforce.

Indeed, I think that WWII was the grand liberator of women; since Western and Soviet men were fighting the Nazis and the Japanese in various theatres of war, women at home had to replace them in factories, schools, administration, and farms. All of a sudden, a woman driving a truck or working at a factory was the new norm, what people were seeing on a daily basis. Working women were no longer considered unlucky losers or ugly ducklings who did not manage to find a husband. The superb Canadian series *Bomb Girls*[4] tells the stories of young women recruited into

---

sophisticated Paris aristocrat Roxane. He writes poetic love letters for his relative Christian, whom Roxane begins to love because of Cyrano's letters. Christian is physically handsome, but hopeless with words. Born with an extraordinarily large nose, Cyrano is physically ugly. He is, in fact, *moche*. Young English rose Jane Birkin (1946–2023) had lovingly called her husband Serge Gainsbourg (1928–1991) *tellement moche*. Yet, unlike Jane, Roxane never loves Cyrano. Shortly before his death, Roxane finds out about his authorship of Christian's letters. Thus, Cyrano is the embodiment of selfless true love. Sonia takes her class hostage because she loves the teenagers, the young human beings. Hers is not the erotic love of Cyrano, but *agape* or the feeling of deep empathy for another human being, in Sonia's case, her class.

[3] Simone de Beauvoir, *The Second Sex* (London: Vintage Books, 2011).
[4] *Bomb Girls* on https://www.imdb.com/title/tt1955311/; accessed 11 February 2024.

the war effort; their lives undergo irreversible changes due to their employment in a bomb factory.

In the first decade after WWII, save for the Soviet Union[5] and her block of satellite states in Central and Eastern Europe, male Western governments were trying to make women go back to their traditional roles of home makers, mothers, and wives. The 1950 films with Doris Day (1922–2019), the all-American blond girl, funny, harmless, and a good sport, portrayed Western societies' wish to re-define the female and her traditional duties after the grand equalizer WWII. The Austrian Sissy films with young Romy Schneider (1938–1982) were box office hits. Why?

Intent on making its enthusiastic and dedicated collaboration with the Nazi slaughter of Europe go away, the Austrian film industry was eager to portray a happy and harmless past. The Austro-Hungarian monarchy (1848–1918)

---

[5] Read Svetlana Alexievich, *The Unwomanly Face of War. An Oral History of Women in World War II* (New York: Random House, 2017). Alexievich portrays the brutal lives of Soviet women and girls during WWII. The excellent Soviet film *A Zory Sdes' Tyxhyie (The Dawns here are Quiet)* from 1972 https://www.imdb.com/title/tt0068161/; accessed 23 February 2024, tells a true story: stationed in the North and commanded by an old man, not exactly a hero of the prestigious Soviet military, a platoon of young women leave for a reconnaissance mission. The old guy is very knowledgeable about the swamps and the territory. Five young women: some of them left university in June 1941, when Nazi Germany attacked the Soviet Union, some left high school, and others were from good Soviet stock, working class. The old man is the only one who survives. The Germans shot four young women, and one died in a swamp, on her way to warn the villagers of the German platoon. This film is unforgettable, and its principal tenets are: the most beautiful landscape can have a brutal past. An old man who looks like a looser teaches young women how to read nature and, lastly, men and women sacrificed their lives defending their country.

was an ideal past: too far back in time to arouse criticism and too idealized a past after the horrors of WWII. Sissy, Empress Elisabeth of Austria (1837–1898) was therefore an ideal and much-needed female figure of identification for Austrian and German girls. The next generation of women should be like Sissy: intelligent, rebellious, disciplined, beautiful, a loyal wife and a loving mother.

1968 was the year of societal emancipation from pre-war traditional roles in Western societies. 1968 cannot be appreciated enough, since that year was a step to more liberty; the Paris, Rome and Berlin student-activists of 1968 demanded the truth, especially in West Germany. Look at the Nazi past of our parents and grandparents with a critical eye. The children and grandchildren of the Nazi generation rebelled; they rejected their ancestors' superficial apologetics and lame whitewashing of the Nazi past. Few of them became terrorists, guided by a mistaken radical view of Soviet-type socialism; groups like the German RAF (Rote Armee Fraktion), the Italian Brigate Rosse (Red Brigades) and French Action Directe (Direct Action) underwent military training in Palestine and Lebanon and returned to Western Europe to change society, ignorant of the wishes of the majority of citizens.

The idea of liberty, political freedom, is intoxicating; once a few courageous persons have inculcated it into the minds of those who listen, it is festering—no way back. After WWII, women were demanding equality in society, since they had proved what they were capable of during the war. The 1960's de-colonialisation movements in Africa and Asia chimed in well with societal liberation in the West, and feminist literature blossomed. Traditional manners and values, such as, e.g. a decent girl marries as a virgin, were no longer attractive to young women. In my humble opinion, feminists of the second wave[6] over-exaggerated the sexual aspect of women's liberation, but I do understand why sex was such an important issue to them. If I am a citizen enjoying equal rights, female by chance, not by choice, neither state nor society can dictate me what to do, with whom I sleep and how I lead my life.

Eventually, it was a man who created the instrument for the final liberation of women from their biological yoke: Carl Djerassi (1923–2015) invented the anticonception pill, thus provided women and men with freedom from unwanted pregnancies.[7] Now, women were able to develop their full intellectual and professional potential.

Academics such as Cambridge classicist Mary Beard (*1955), Philadelphian art historian Camille Paglia (*1947) and German born New York philosopher Hannah Arendt are but the most prominent role models of women in science and academe. Today, the world benefits from female doctors, teachers, engineers, and politicians. Yet, what about the unfinished female, the girl, the female teenager? What role does the girl have in society, or rather, what role should it have? What did de Beauvoir think about female teenagers,

---

[6] https://www.gale.com/primary-sources/womens-studies/collections/second-wave-feminism#:~:text=The%20second%20wave%20feminism%20movement,spread%20to%20other%20Western%20countries; accessed 28 January 2024.

[7] https://www.nytimes.com/2015/02/01/us/carl-djerassi-dies-at-91-forever-altered-reproductive-practices-as-a-creator-of-the-pill.html; accessed 28 January 2024.

and how does the film *Skirt Day* portray them? Let us now have a look at *La Journée de la Jupe*, a French film produced by arte France and affiliated European film institutions in 2008.

La Journée de la Jupe (Skirt Day)

A normal school day at a Paris high school, a *lycée*. Sonia Bergerac arrives; she is an attractive black-haired white lady in her mid-forties. The divine Isabelle Adjani (*1955) portrays her to perfection.[8] Bergerac wears a brown skirt, knee-length black boots, a white blouse, and a beige blazer. She is slim and beautiful, but one can see anxiety in her face. The teenagers are wearing unisex gear: sweatpants, t-shirts, sports jackets, and expensive sneakers. The girls are wearing sports trousers or jeans, and not one is wearing a skirt, *une jupe*.

The entire class is late, and obviously, the teenagers do respect neither their teacher nor the class schedule. The pupils enter the school's theatre room, and we see Bergerac swallow some pills. The pupils are loud and uninterested, frequently shouting the p word.[9] Bergerac shouts at them repeatedly, but her intensive and almost hysterical 'Taisez vous! (Be quiet)' has no effect. The pupils are making fun of the comedy-ballet they should have prepared for today: Jean-Baptiste Molière's *Le Bourgeois Gentilhomme* (1670).

---

[8] Isabelle Adjani is the only French *comédienne* who has won 5 Césars, the French equivalent to the US Oscar: https://www.isabelleadjani.fr; accessed 13 February 2024.

[9] The French equivalent to the English f word is the p word: p as in *putain*, a vulgar expression I do not wish to translate here.

Bergerac calls up two boys to rehearse a scene on stage: their lack of enthusiasm and disinterest is visible, and that the class is making fun of them does not help. The viewer pities Bergerac, since normal instruction with these feral teenagers is an impossible task—they seem to be immune against the most basic principles of school discipline: shut up and listen, watch, and learn. When two of the most obnoxious male teenagers, one of them is Mouss, a black Muslim, meet behind a wall, Bergerac goes after them, wanting to know what they are doing. A revolver falls out of one of the boy's *sac à dos* (rucksack)—and Bergerac, shocked, grabs it.

This is a pivotal scene: we see Sonia, a dedicated *prof de français*, holding a gun—and in this very moment, she immediately grasps her new strength.[10] The revolver is a

---

[10] I follow Hannah Arendt's definitions of power, strength, authority, and violence, in *On Violence* (New York: Harvest 1970), 44-46. "*Power* corresponds to the human ability not just to act but to act in concert. Power is never the property of an individual; it belongs to a group and remains in existence only so long as the group keeps together. When we say of somebody that he is 'in power' we actually refer to his being empowered by a certain number of people to act in their name." "*Strength* unequivocally designates something in the singular, an individual entity; it is the property inherent in an object or person and belongs to its character, which may prove itself in relation to other things or persons, but is essentially independent of them. The strength of even the strongest individual can always be overpowered by the many [...]" "*Authority* [...] can be vested in persons [...] or it can be vested in offices, as, for instance, in the Roman senate (*auctoritas in senatu*) or in the hierarchical offices of the Church [...] Its hallmark is unquestioning recognition by those who are asked to obey; neither coercion nor persuasion is needed. [...] To remain in authority requires respect for the person or the office. The greatest enemy of authority, therefore, is contempt, and the surest way to undermine it is laughter." "*Violence*, finally [...] is distinguished by its instrumental

prolongation of Bergerac's physical strength, thus a tool of violence. Now, the pupils are afraid of her, all the more so as she has just hit alpha boy Mouss in the leg by accident, when he tried to grab the gun from her. The wound is harmless, but the class is now obeying her. They all lie down on the floor, with hands behind their heads. Sonia is in total command. Thanks to the gun, she has now also the authority every teacher in normal conditions enjoys.

"This time, I won't cave in!"[11] she shouts, and we understand her: the daily frustration of trying to teach the obnoxious teenagers, her enthusiasm for French literature and her dedication to education. She is in an impossible situation: the principal is a coward, incapable of protecting his teachers. He hides behind some misunderstood ideological principles of multiculturalism. A principal's task is to steer the school, to keep up standards of studying, to make sure that the pupils shall achieve the *baccalauréat*, a certificate required to enrol at a French university. But this principal is not up to his job.

Sonia locks the door, while the principal is meeting the special force of the Paris police that has just arrived. Béchet, the commander of the special force, has to deal with a rebellious officer. Captain Labouret is the team's negotiator, and as an experienced police officer, he advises not to escalate the situation. Let's just talk to her, I am sure we can find a solution.

---

character. Phenomenologically, it is close to strength, since the implements of violence, like all other tools, are designed and used for the purpose of multiplying natural strength [...]"

[11] 0:8:56.

Labouret engages in reconnaissance, asking Sonia's colleagues about her psychological state of mind. A female teacher tells him that Sonia, her friend, had repeatedly told the principal about the difficult situation, but the principal did nothing. No, Sonia Bergerac is no racist; she just wants to keep up school discipline and the high level of education. And yes, Sonia takes the liberty to wear skirt. So what? A male teacher tells Labouret that he is keeping up the pupils' discipline with teaching the Quran, and the viewer immediately identifies him as a weakling, kissing up to the Muslim alpha boys.

Employed at a French public *lycée*, this teacher's task would be to uphold laicism that separates religion from instruction. Religion has nothing to do with education—that was the rationale of 1789. The *lycée* is a state school. One of the modernizing results of the French Revolution and the *Code Napoléon* or *Code Civil Des Français (1804)*[12] was the French education system. *Liberté, égalité, fraternité* thus meant that French *citoyens* were free from aristocratic or Church bonds, equal in front of the newly established law system, and the nation was like an extended family.

---

[12] https://www.napoleon.org/enseignants/documents/le-code-civil-21-mars-1804-naissance-principes-et-posterite/#:~:text=ans%20à%20aboutir.-,Le%20Code%20civil%20des%20Français%20fut%20promulgué%20le%2021%20mars,pénal%20(sanction%20des%20infractions); accessed 17 February 2024. Article 2 refers to the "non-confessionalité de l'État, point de depart de la laicité française", thus the state's neutrality in religious matters. This promoted civil marriage and the end of the discrimination of the Jews. For the original text see https://www.assemblee-nationale.fr/evenements/code-civil-1804-1.asp; accessed 17 February 2024.

This powerful idea, a blend of Enlightenment ideas, put forward by Kant, Voltaire and Rousseau, and nationalism in its infant shoes established the state's compulsory school system. All children were to enjoy basic education. Why? Because only state-controlled compulsory education could grant critical thinking (Kant), act as intellectual bulwark against Catholic superstitious dogmata (Voltaire), establish the consciousness of one's rights as a French citizen (Napoleon) and, hopefully, inculcate the rational thought that everybody can liberate himself by studying (Rousseau). To be free, equal and a brother or a sister thus also meant what the Americans would refer to as 'the pursuit of happiness', to steer one's life toward one's goals. And these goals were subjective goals, personal wishes, and individual aspirations.

Thus, what Kant, Voltaire and Rousseau considered enlightenment, *Aufklärung,* had very much to do with education. If I, a nine-year old kid, cannot go to school because I have to labour in a coal mine so my family can eat, I won't be able to develop a critical mind, because I cannot read or do basic mathematics. I am illiterate, a slave to my employers until the day I die—and that was the basic and mistaken idea of Karl Marx, who saw only oppression, but not the chances Capitalism offered, namely, the individual's opportunities and choices in a free market.

When Sonia criticizes the contemptuous and misogynistic attitude of the Arab boys towards the girls, most of them also being of Arabic descent, one of the girls asks her if she is Jewish? The girl implies that Bergerac hates Muslims.

Sonia replies: "I won't answer this question. This is a laic school."[13] She adds that in France, racism is punished by law.

The situation's dangerous potential for a massacre develops when the minister of education arrives; as politician responsible for the school system, she has to defend her reputation and naturally, wants to be re-appointed again. If she botches this job, her career is *fini*. She advises commander Béchet to storm the drama room in an hour if negotiator Labouret cannot talk Bergerac into surrender. In the meantime, Labouret talks to Sonia's ex-husband, who confirms the female teacher's view: the principal has failed to react to Sonia's repeated warnings. He has done nothing.

In the drama room, Sonia is lecturing; for the first time, the pupils are listening, learning that being a member of a theatre group in Molière's time one did not enjoy celebrity status. On the contrary: back then, pre-revolutionary French society considered actors and, especially actresses, as criminals and whores, as social outcasts. Why? Because they did not attend regular Church service, due to their profession as travelling *comédiens*. In some of the girls' faces, we can observe the beginning of an understanding, an inkling of what it means to be equal to the boys.

Sonia's dedication to the teenagers is visible when she appeals to their reason: their parents immigrated to France so they would have a better life. She is exhausted and sad: "Your only chance is to work hard at school."[14]

---

[13] 00:36:22.
[14] 00:45:54.

In a tired moment, Sonia is unattentive, and Mouss attacks her, throws her on the floor and punches her in the face. Sonia loses the gun and Nawal, a blond girl, picks it up. She is now in command. Looking at a mobile phone—Sonia had the class place their phones on a desk, when she got the gun—the blond girl finds a video clip: it displays the gang rape of Farida, an obese Arab girl. The rapists are three of her classmates. So shocked is Nawal that she asks Farida why she never talked about this. The girls are crying together, and once Sonia has escaped Mouss, Nawal returns the gun to Sonia.

This is a sign of trust, since Nawal, in a strong position because of the gun, could have easily made Madame Bergerac unlock the door and free the class—but she gives Sonia the gun, thus demonstrating that she respects her teacher's authority. Sonia sends the clip to Labouret who immediately issues arrest warrants for the rapists. When Labouret calls Sonia again, asking what she wants, she tells him:

> "I want my message to be broadcast on all major news outlets and the state to confirm that it will arrange for an annual *journée de la jupe*, a day that demonstrates that one can wear a skirt to school without being regarded as a whore! You have two hours."[15]

This is not only a feminist demand, but also an expression of French enlightenment: men and women are equal in front of the law, but that does not mean that I, a woman, have to

---

[15] 1:00:33.

dress like a man. In a free and tolerant society, I must have a choice. Sonia's demand for the skirt day is therefore a homage to the liberty and equality of French women and girls. Indirectly, Sonia's demand is also a criticism of the social manners of the Muslim pupils, who are treating their female classmates as inferior sex. Sonia's *journée de la jupe* is not an act of the hatred of Muslims, but an affirmation of France's liberty of all. When Labouret gets Sonia's parents on the phone, the teenagers learn that she is also of Arabic descent. She says good-bye to her parents in Arabic. The teenagers are shocked, asking her why she never told them. She replies that her origins do not matter, she is *prof de français*.

The boy Mehmed, one of the rapists—Mouss has told Sonia a couple of minutes ago who the rapists are—gets the gun and calls Labouret: he should send an airplane and one million US dollars. Some teenagers attack him, and Mehmed shoots a boy. The police raid the drama room, and Sonia defends Mehmed: it was her who killed the boy. In the chaos, Sonia is staying on, much like the captain of a sinking ship; she could have run into safety, but she is intent of protecting the teenagers. She is shot, by accident. The teenagers escape and fall into the arms of their parents who have been waiting the whole day at the school.

The final scene is most touching: we see a cemetery with the French *tricolore*. Sonia's parents and an Imam are standing at the grave, quietly praying in Arabic. Slowly, girls and boys are joining them: Sonia's pupils. All girls are wearing *jupe,* throwing roses on to Sonia's grave. They are fulfilling Sonia's wish, paying their respects to their teacher who only wanted their freedom and equality, whose compassion had been trying to convince them to understand that education is important, especially for children of a linguistic, cultural, and religious minority. They have understood the message: the *jupe* is Sonia Bergerac's symbol of female liberty and equality, and her death in the drama room her last act of love for her pupils.

This film, rather ignored by international film critics, is a drama only the French can pull off: intense, innovative, interesting, courageous, full of humour in even the most brutal scenes, honest, elegant, and never obscene. We can feel with Sonia, her despair about the chaotic conditions at the school, quiet suffering, and love for her teenagers.

Instead of a Conclusion: Simone de Beauvoir's Girl

The female teenager is an unfinished woman, dominated by her parents and society's expectations:

> "As she is already detached from her childhood past, the present is for her only a transition; she sees no valid ends in it, only occupations. In a more or less disguised way, her youth is consumed by waiting. She is waiting for Man. [...] For the girl, erotic transcendence consists in making herself prey in order to make a catch. She becomes an object; and she grasps herself as object."[16]

De Beauvoir's criticism of Western societies' misogyny was probably accurate in 1949, when her study was first published. Back then, as I have said before, society had clear expectations for women: one had to be decent, obedient,

---

[16] De Beauvoir, 352, 360.

and pure, waiting to find a wealthy and successful man to marry and have healthy children. In the late 1980s and early 1990s, there was saying in my country: *stud marriage*. It referred to young women who attended university, studying easy subjects such as French, German literature or Spanish. These students had allegedly chosen these easy subjects for one reason: to meet a young man and get married. Fewer girls than boys pursued the difficult subjects such as civil engineering, medicine, history, the classics, or chemistry.

Today, I do not see a big difference in the upbringing of boys and girls in our Western societies. There are, of course, gender-related ways of education, but girls are enjoying sports, can wear what they like, are no longer considered the weaker sex, and are promoted to succeed in whatever profession they choose. Especially female physicians are very much appreciated, also by male patients, since they recognize that female doctors are often more understanding and kinder than alpha male doctors.

As a teacher in a secondary school and at two universities, I can say that the girls, boys and young adults are being treated equally; often, the teenage girls are more ambitious than the boys. They often work harder at school and most of them have a good sense of self; they are neither weaklings nor wallflowers. All my female students have clear plans for their future, and, at university, pregnant students and young mothers are very rare exceptions.

Yet, one aspect of being female shall remain: the biological faculty of bearing children. Therefore, de Beauvoir was spot on when she, back in the 1950s, observed women's willingness to sacrifice their plans for marriage and children:

> "People are often surprised to see how easily a woman gives up music, studies or a job as soon as she has found a husband; this is because she had committed too little of herself to her projects to derive benefit from their accomplishment."[17]

Today, I think de Beauvoir's view does no longer apply to the situation of young women in the Western world. To give up one's profession for love? Sacrifice my independence for a partner? I think that today's young women would just laugh at that idea. They are experiencing the personal satisfaction of professional life daily: earning one's own money, driving a car I have paid for with my own money, meeting friends at restaurants are aspects of quality of life. I am convinced that young women today would not exchange their financial independence for marriage. My female teenagers at the secondary school might not yet have specific plans for their future, but not one told me that she aspires to be a housewife and mother—and that is a smashing success of feminism. Naturally, women's biological clock is ticking, but the decision to procreate is a choice of both women and men. This will never change.

Therefore, I think that feminism, and I mean here, true feminism that recognizes duties and rights, and not the whiny shouty hypocritical pseudo-feminism of the 'Believe all women' gang, has, indeed, succeeded. We are in 2024, and all my female friends are educated. They are doctors, designers, diplomats, lawyers, assistants, and teachers, and all of them are earning good salaries. Therefore,

---

[17] De Beauvoir, 393.

independence is the most important aspect of feminism. Most of my friends have children, and most of them are bringing them up in the spirit of equality. In the West, women have achieved equality and liberty, but, unfortunately, in many countries in Africa, Asia and South America, ancient societal patterns of misogyny still rule. To women and men in these countries, Kant's famous saying should be a guiding principle:

> "Enlightenment is man's emergence from his self-imposed immaturity. Immaturity is the inability to use one's understanding without guidance from another."[18]

---

[18] https://www.goodreads.com/quotes/246637-enlightenment-is-man-s-emergence-from-his-self-imposed-immaturity-immaturity-is; accessed 18 February 2024. The original German: "Aufklärung ist der Ausgang des Menschen aus seiner selbst verschuldeten Unmündigkeit. Unmündigkeit ist das Unvermögen, sich seines Verstandes ohne Leitung eines anderen zu bedienen." The entire text on https://www.goodreads.com/quotes/246637-enlightenment-is-man-s-emergence-from-his-self-imposed-immaturity-immaturity-is ; accessed 18 February 2024.

III. Immanuel Kant's Perpetual War: *Fauda*

"'The Perpetual Peace'. A Dutch innkeeper once put this satirical inscription on his signboard, along with the picture of a graveyard."[1]

Immanuel Kant's (1724–1804) famous treatise *On Perpetual Peace* (1795) suggested what states should do when planning to enter peace negotiations with the goal to conclude a peace that would last.

To begin peace negotiations, I can identify two situations: first, I am losing, running out of weapons and soldiers. The enemy's army is stronger, has better weapons and a better strategy, more money to buy more weapons and more allies supportive of its cause. Second, both our armies, soldiers, and the civilian population alike, are equally exhausted; we are locked in a stalemate. So, we both agree to end hostilities. In the first case, my generals tell me that peace negotiations are now the only solution to end the people's misery and save as much of my territory; it is therefore rational to enter peace negotiations as long as I have the possibility to negotiate.

In case two, a stalemate, it is to both our interest to end the hostilities, save lives and conclude a peace or a ceasefire. Yet, if I carry on the hostilities, knowing that I am losing, the consequences of my ruthlessness will prompt a cruel future for my people: unconditional surrender. Loss of honour,

---

[1] Kant, *Political Writings*, ed. by H. S. Reiss (Cambridge: Cambridge University Press, 1991 (2)), 93.

respect, trust, and faith, in domestic and international relations. I think that unconditional surrender is, in psychological terms, more damaging to my people and my army than a peace treaty in which I have a saying as a partner.

The allies in WWII brought Nazi Germany and Japan to their knees with unconditional surrender. What followed was the subsequent occupation of Japan and West Germany by the Allied Forces. Occupation by a foreign force will change the occupied nation's culture and thinking about itself.

Kant, the genius from Königsberg, today's Kaliningrad, described the conditions necessary for peace, thereby differentiating between peace and ceasefire. Ceasefire is the silencing of the weapons to gain time required to rebuild one's army, stock up on weaponry and reconsider one's strategy. As an adherent of the political system of a republic, Kant promoted the most ethical argument: the civilian population that suffers most from war should decide when and why their state goes to war, because they carry the financial, psychological, and political burden.

We could thus call Kant's famous treatise a text that aimed, in a very general sense, at democratisation in domestic affairs and foreign policy, because, prior to the French Revolution of 1789, only kings, sultans, tsars, and emperors decided about war and peace. The exception was *La Serenissima* that had developed a political system unusual for her times:

> "The hinterland was lost in fire and vengeance. Driven by barbarism, brutality [...] the peoples of the Veneto cities abandoned their comforts and fled into their

obvious refuge—the lagoon. [...] Guided by priests and patricians of the old order, they devised new institutions based upon Roman precedents; there were governing tribunes in each settlement, slowly uniting, with bickering and bloodshed, into a single administration under the presidency of a non-hereditary Doge, elected for life—'rich and poor under equal laws' [...] 'This Venice, which we have raised in the lagoon, is our mighty habitation, and no power of Emperor or Prince can touch us.'"[2]

An elected Doge ruled Venice; the city was financially successful because *La Serenissima* traded with everyone, pragmatically accumulating wealth. The Doge's position was non-hereditary, which made sure that no powerful family could usurp political rule for itself and its offspring. Furthermore, to make the swamp land of the lagoon habitable and ready for agriculture was egalitarian labour, as there were no property rights yet on the swamp. To make the land arable for people and cattle was therefore a democratic exercise: everybody worked for the land as they were all refugees. Marco Polo (1254–1324) was a splendid example for Venice's tolerance of other cultures;[3] he travelled to Asia and his account of what he saw there has become our Western civilization's view of that part of the world.

In her times, Venice's political system was egalitarian and proto-democratic, when compared with the European

---

[2] The best book about Venice and her history is Jan Morris, *Venice* (London: faber & faber, 1993 (3)), 5, 6.
[3] Marco Polo on https://www.britannica.com/biography/Marco-Polo; accessed 22 September 2023.

monarchs' authoritarian and absolutist rule, for example, Henry VIII (1491–1547), and Louis XIV (1638–1715), France's *roi soleil*. Election of the Doge until the day he dies allows me, a member of the aristocracy, to scrutinize the candidates, while the non-hereditary character of the position is a safeguard against nepotism and corruption.

Since her foundation, Israel has been a parliamentary democracy, a rule-of-law state, and an ally of the West. Much like Venice, the state was founded by refugees and immigrants, who did *aliya* (ascent, or going up);[4] some arrived in Palestine in the last decades of the 19th and early decades of the 20th century, while others found refuge as survivors of the Holocaust after 1945. Mostly Jews from Eastern Europe fled to Palestine in the first waves of *aliya*, because of the antisemitism in their home countries. They were also Zionists,[5] eager to create Theodor Herzl's (1860–1904) Jewish state that would end the diaspora. Golda Meir (1898–1978) was born in Kiev, today's Ukraine, as Golda Mabovich, and David Ben-Gurion (1896–1973) was born

---

[4] There are five waves of *aliya*: 1882 to 1903; 1904-1914; 1919-1923; 1924-1931, and 1932-1938. After WWII, immigration to Palestine was legal and illegal (*aliya bet*), because of the restrictions issued by the British who held the mandate of Palestine. After 1989, the limited liberalization in the Soviet Union and her republics, which, on a wider political framework also affected Ethiopia, 750,000 Jews immigrated to Israel; Bernard Reich and David H. Goldberg, *Historical Dictionary of Israel. Second edition* (Lanham, Maryland: The Scarecrow Press, Inc., 2008), 32-33.

[5] On Herzl as the founder of Zionism see https://www.britannica.com/biography/Theodor-Herzl; accessed 4 October 2023. Superb in its brevity and precise explanation is Steven Beller, *Antisemitism. A Very Short Introduction* (Oxford: Oxford University Press, 2007).

David Gruen in Płońsk, today's Poland, back then the Russian Empire.

In this essay, I shall apply Kant's principles of perpetual peace to the plots of the very successful Israeli TV series *Fauda* (*Chaos*).[6] In chapter 1, I introduce Kant's six preliminary articles, explaining their importance for the beginning of peace negotiations. Chapter 2 introduces the series *Fauda*, its most important characters and two narrative themes or plots: first, I scrutinize the anti-terror unit and the professional and private lives of its members, families, and friends, as portrayed in series 1 and 2. Second, I analyse the most dangerous terrorist threat the unit has to fight, superbly portrayed in series 4.[7] In the conclusion, I shall inquire whether Kant's principles can be applied to *Fauda*. Can we with Kant explain why a lasting peace between the Palestinians and the Israelis is not realistic in the near future?[8] Are Palestinians and Israelis condemned to perpetual war, and if so, why?

---

[6] All information about the series' episodes, actors, reception, and planned production can be found on https://www.imdb.com/title/tt4565380/; accessed 19 September 2023. Interesting information about the series on https://jewishunpacked.com/fauda-the-true-story-behind-the-chaos/; accessed 21 September 2023.

[7] At the time of writing, series 5 is in the making, thus the story of Doron and his anti-terrorist unit continues.

[8] Note that I am no specialist in the Palestinian-Israeli conflict in the Gaza strip and the West Bank with the cities Jenin, Ramallah, and Hebron since I neither speak Hebrew nor Arabic. I recommend consulting various news channels: BBC International, Jerusalem Post, Haaretz, Al Jazeera, Neue Zürcher Zeitung and others.

I. Kant's six preliminary articles

To prepare the grounds for peace negotiations, thus preconditions, Kant defined six preliminary principles[9] that should be understood as prohibitive laws (*leges prohibitivae*), hence laws that forbid me to do something or act in a specific way. Therefore, I must fulfil these six principles prior to entering the room where peace negotiations are scheduled to be hold.

First: "No conclusion of peace shall be considered valid as such if it was made with a secret reservation of the material for a future war." This means that if I prepare for peace negotiations, I must mean it; I must be willing to make peace. I cannot enter peace negotiations with a secret reservation (*reservatio mentalis*), planning to carry on the hostilities once I will have stocked up on weaponry or have recruited more soldiers. Such secret reservation or concealed plan will prompt only a truce, not peace, and if I sign a peace treaty with a concealed plan to carry on hostilities at a later point in time, I break the treaty before it is signed, betraying the other negotiation party. The consequence of such a decision is the loss of trust. Why would my adversary trust me in the future, enter peace negotiations with me in the future? Therefore, principle 1 is of immediate effect and cannot be postponed.

Second: "No independently existing state, whether it be large or small, may be acquired by another state by inheritance, exchange, purchase or gift." If we replace the words 'independently existing' with 'sovereign', we learn

---

[9] Kant, 93-96.

that the second principle protects the future of a sovereign state. The political system does not matter, regardless of who rules, be it an absolute monarchy, i.e. Russia ruled by the Tsars; a constitutional monarchy, i.e. Great Britain today; a republic, i.e. the American Republic founded in 1776; or a confederation, i.e. Switzerland since 1848. No government is allowed to breach his state's sovereignty by selling the state or parts of it, give it to one's relatives as a gift or exchange its territory for a territory elsewhere. Why? Because the state, its constitution, administration, and institutions, is not a property (*patrimonium*), while its territory is. I can buy land in the beautiful state of Louisiana in the South of the USA and build a house there, but I cannot buy Louisiana state institutions, such as the tax office. This principle further implies to me that Kant was also thinking about the state's inhabitants, citizens, or subjects. If my king can sell the state I am a subject of, what rights do I have? Even if my king does not acknowledge human rights, I am at least protected as subject of my state, with concomitant property and inheritance rights and a political identity. This second principle can be postponed and dealt with at a later point in time.

Third: "Standing armies (*miles perpetuus*) will gradually be abolished altogether." In Kant's times, standing, regular armies were expensive and posed a threat to other states. Once the peace treaty has been signed, my former adversary and I can begin to reduce our armies or abolish them altogether. This third principle can be postponed, as it does not require immediate action. It can be dealt with after the signing of the peace treaty.

Fourth: "No national debt shall be contracted in connection with the external affairs of the state." If state B owes me, state A, money, I have a reason to collect this debt by means of war. An international credit system can be a source of war; therefore, it should be abolished. This third principle can be postponed; the regulation of international finance, loans and debts can be solved by stipulations we agree upon in the peace treaty.

Fifth: "No state shall forcibly interfere in the constitution and government of another state." If I, state A, send troops to state B to have its constitution changed, unseat its ruler, and establish a ruler of my preference, or if I influence state B's relations with states C and D, I am at war, breaking the peace. This fifth principle protects the legitimacy and legal status of a sovereign state and its foreign and domestic politics. State B's domestic affairs and foreign relations are his sovereign rights. This principle cannot be postponed; it is a crucial pre-condition of a lasting peace. Here again, we can observe how Kant valued sovereignty as the most important feature of a state.

Sixth: "No state at war with another shall permit such acts of hostility as would make mutual confidence impossible during a future time of peace. Such acts would include the employment of assassins (*percussores*) or poisoners (*venefici*), breach of agreements, the instigation of treason (*perduellio*) within the enemy state, etc." The sending of spies and terrorists to the enemy's territory, cities and towns are destroying trust, even when I, state A, am at war with state B. Is highly unlikely that state B will enter peace negotiations with me, because of my hostile activities. Note that Kant explicitly speaks of activities that have nothing to do with the theatre of war, when army A confronts army B. He explicitly says that any activities outside of the theatre of war, that is, besides military operations, are eroding trust, because the target of these secret operations is the civilian sector of the state. Kant, rather idealistically, it seems to me, anticipated that information gathering, a much-needed tool in warfare, would breach trust, thus rendering peace negotiations null and void. This sixth principle is of immediate effect and cannot be postponed.

II a.   The Team is the Family, *Fauda* series 1 and 2

The first episode of series 1 begins with an idyllic portrait of a seemingly happy family: Former special forces operative Doron Kavilio, superbly portrayed by Lior Raz, owns a wine yard and is married to beautiful wife Gali, played by Neta Garty. The couple has a boy called Ido and daughter Noga. Gali is unhappy in the marriage and begins an affair with Doron's team colleague Naor, portrayed by Tsahi Halevy; at the end of series 1, the Kavilios are divorced. Yet, Gali is always there for Doron when he is depressed or desperate. She is a loyal ex-wife.

Doron is tending to his wines when he sees a person approaching. It is Michael 'Mickey' Moreno, his former commander-in-chief, who wants him back for one operation: the panther is alive, and Doron is the only one who can identify him. Doron is puzzled; he is convinced that he has witnessed the death of Abu Ahmad, portrayed by Hisham Suliman. Yet Moreno, played by Yuval Segal, knows how to pull the strings on Doron's professional pride, noticing that his former fighter is rather bored on the farm. His wine business is not doing well. Doron begins training and joins his old special forces team, happy to be back—and so is the team. They are Shin Bet (*Shabak*),[10] and all speak Arabic, a requirement for their undercover operations in Gaza and the West Bank. We sense that the team is bound by psychological ties that are like family relations, full of trust, loyalty, friendship, respect, and appreciation, but also temper, anger and aggression. The team members know each other so well that they are forgiving. Everyone loses his temper, gets aggressive or uses foul language—that comes with the stressful job.

Series 1 tells the story of how the team liquidates Abu Ahmad, a radical Hamas member who has killed 116 Israelis, among them children and elderly citizens. The team kidnaps Abu Ali when he is praying at a mosque. We meet Gabi aka Captain Ayub, played by Itzik Cohen; he is a superb psychologist and always knows what to do to gather information in interrogations. He appeals to an individual's fear of being exposed to Hamas as a traitor, uses blackmail by threatening to expose a person's extra-marital sexual activities or sexual orientation, and offers, on the other hand, medical treatment for sick Palestinian children, or passports to leave Palestine for good. He is also ruthless in using family relations to get close to an individual who can provide the team with information. Gabi offers Abu Ali a deal: Tell me

---

[10] Acronym for Sherut Bitahon Klali, General Security Services. Shin Bet's tasks is to prevent hostile secret activities on Israel's territory, including espionage and sabotage. It was founded in 1948; Reich and Goldberg, 463.

what Abu Ahmad is up to, and I'll arrange for an eye operation for your daughter Nadia. Abu Ali reveals that he has heard that Abu Ahmad has smuggled the nerve gas Sarin into the West Bank.

Doron and Eli, portrayed by Yakov Zada Daniel, disguise themselves as employees of a Palestinian bakery that delivers sweets to the wedding of Abu Ahmad's younger brother Bashir who is marrying beautiful Amal. The plan is to eliminate Abu Ahmad when he shows up at the wedding. Yet, one of the party guests has an inkling, observing Doron and Eli who are serving sweets. He asks Doron and Eli to identify themselves and, after interrogating them, he finally believes their story; they arrived late because they were held up at the border check point. In a second, Doron loses his self-control and shoots the interrogator; they shoot their way out, shouting *Fauda*, the key word for HQ to extract them. The team members carry ear devices and have drones filming them; they are in steady contact with HQ.

Had Doron kept his cool, they could have walked out peacefully, probably spotted Abu Ahmad in the street, and eliminated him quietly there. But Doron's instinct for survival is lightning fast, visceral. Abu Ahmad is about to enter the wedding in disguise when Doron recognizes him. Chasing him through the dark streets of the village, Doron shoots Abu Ahmad in the back. In the chaos of them fleeing the wedding, Boaz, Doron's brother-in-law, shoots groom Bashir. The pace is set for the principal theme of *Fauda*: revenge and retaliation, a never-ending cycle of violence. An eye for an eye, a tooth for a tooth. If you kill my brother, I will kill your's. To break this cycle, this pattern of behaviour, requires trust on both sides, the willingness to forgive and enter a compromise to make the ceasefire work.

In seconds, Bashir and Amal's wedding has turned into Bashir's funeral; the death of her soon-to-be husband has politicized and radicalized Amal. When a young man finds matches with the logo of Tel Aviv bar San Bernard Boaz has lost in the shoot-out, the viewer knows that the bar will be the next target of Hamas.

Back home in Tel Aviv, the team sits on the veranda of HQ, smoking, drinking and relaxing. We often see them sitting there after an operation, winding down with heavy drinking and smoking, and who could reproach them those brief moments of peace and quiet? The veranda is like a family living room to them. Boaz is on the way to San Bernard, where his girlfriend, beautiful blond Daria, is working. When Doron, late at night, fills bottles with his white wine, Gali joins him in the barn. She asks him to leave everything behind and emigrate; she fears that Doron will re-join the team for more operations in the future. He had left to save the marriage, but Moreno and Gabi have pulled him back in.

Boaz and Daria sit with Gali, smoking pot; the young couple is in love, and Gali is happy for her little brother. Sheikh Avdallah, a respected elderly Hamas leader, visits the grieving family. Amal wants revenge. HQ finds out that Abu Ahmad might have been brought to Nablus hospital and sends Doron for reconnaissance. There, Doron meets Dr Shirin El Abed, portrayed by Letitia Eido. Shirin is the cousin of Walid, a young follower of Abu Ahmad. She studied medicine in Paris and came back home to the West Bank to be with her mother. While Abu Ahmad is being brought to a safe place, leaving the hospital in an ambulance, members of Abu Ahmad's terrorist group are instructing Amal how to place a bag with a bomb at the bar San Bernardo.

It is Nurit's first day as a field operative; the ambitious young woman, portrayed by Rona-Lee Shimon, is nervous. She has the task to follow Shirin to the swimming pool and make a copy of her mobile phone to find out how she is connected to Abu Ahmad via Walid, her cousin. Nurit cannot make a copy as Shirin takes her phone to the shower. Doron waits for his 'sister' Nurit in front of the swimming hall and introduces himself to Shirin as Amir Mahajne, a member of the Palestinian Preventive Security. He is flirting with her, copying her phone number into his phone. Shirin is quite flattered. The viewer learns that she is a lonely widow. Her young husband died of an incurable illness, back in France. Her mother wishes her to be happy again with a new partner.

Boaz arrives at the San Bernardo when the bomb Amal has brought in explodes. So grief-stricken is Amal that she does not leave, ignoring her instructions. She dies in the explosion. Boaz survives and finds Daria's body. Her cruel death changes him forever. In the meantime, Doron/Amir asks Shirin out for a date, and they meet at the popular *Café au lait* in Ramallah.

Gabi interrogates Abu Ahmad's wife Nassrin, who grew up in Germany. Nassrin and Abu Ahmad have two small children. This is the first of many times we witness how cleverly Gabi influences persons, almost crawling into their minds. Such psychological acumen requires empathy, the capability and willingness to put myself in somebody else's mind, to understand the concerns of my enemy. Gabi reminds Nassrin of the peace in her native Germany, and how happy her children would be there, far away from the violence ruling in the West Bank. Nassrin rejects Gabi's arguments, insisting that everybody knows that the panther is dead and that she would never betray the father of her children, but Gabi has successfully planted his emotional and reasonable temptation into her mind. Her doubts and wishes are festering, taking on form, chipping slowly away at her loyalty to her husband and his cause. Nassrin, in fear of Hamas and her suspicious mother-in-law, begins to trust Captain Ayub.

Abu Ali wants to meet Abu Ahmad; he should help him clear his name and restore his reputation. People are suspicious of him, thinking that he is collaborating with the Jews. He doesn't know that the team has its drones on to him and leads them to the meeting point. Abu Ahmad's men catch Boaz, and, once again, Abu Ahmad escapes. The team now has not only to deal with having lost Boaz to Hamas; it has to find and liquidate Abu Ahmad before he launches Sarin-loaded bombs into Israel, targeting the civilian population. Time as a stress factor is most brutal, not only for the team in the field, but also the responsible commanders at HQ.

What then develops is superb screenwriting: logical in psychological terms, and, due to the overbearing rationality of revenge, series 1 ends in a cruel denouement. If I have properly understood the plot, and if the *Fauda* plots are close to the reality of the daily life of Israeli special forces, I think that there are three key principles that define the conflict.

First, the team's task is to protect the state of Israel and its citizens from acts of terror. Shin Bet is Israel's domestic secret service. Second, the Palestinian people are represented by the Palestinian authority, a political institution, and various terrorist groups. The PLO is no longer the only group representing the liberation movement; Hamas and Hezbollah are financed by Syria, Lebanon, Qatar, and Iran. Third, owing to the financial power of Hamas, and in series 2 Isis (Daesh), the Palestinian people do not have much of a choice. If they refuse to cooperate with Hamas, or just try to adapt and work as Israeli citizens of Arab descent in Israel, they will be drawn into the conflict because of their family relations. To the team, the family relations of its adversaries are the most important source of information, making possible the planning and execution of operations. From the perspective of the Palestinians, family relations are equally important for the gathering of information. The biblical 'an eye for an eye' is therefore the *modus operandi* of both parties in the conflict, with one crucial exception, convincingly explained by Doron.[11]

The team returns to HQ without Boaz, who is the unit's Benjamin. When Defence Minister Gideon Avitai, played by Uri Gavriel, meets the team to be briefed about what has just happened, Doron is shouting at him, blaming him for his unwillingness to allow for covert retaliation. Minister Avitai: "Israel is a state of civil law, not a terrorist organisation!" Doron: "So rise above the law. Think like an Arab!"[12] Needless

---

[11] Doron explains that difference in S2:E12.
[12] S1:E6.

to say that the minister does not hold Doron in high regard. Avitai thinks that Kavilio is a loose cannon that must be disciplined.

Hamas fighters abduct Shirin and force her to operate on Boaz, blackmailing her with her mother they are holding captive. Doron comes up with a plan to save his little brother-in-law. Naor is the only team member who refuses to go along, voicing his protest: HQ knows nothing about Doron's operation, which makes it an act of mutiny. In legal terms, Naor is right, but he is also motivated by his love for Gali, Doron's wife, has thus personal motives. Steve, portrayed by Doron Ben-David, reveals to Nurit that his first name is Herzl. He, Nurit, Eli and Avihai, played by Boaz Konforty, are all with Doron.

The team abducts elderly Sheikh Avdallah, hide him in a compound and torture him until he reveals Abu Ahmad's hiding place. To treat the elderly sheikh's hands with a hammer is certainly not nice, but the pain prompts results: Sheikh Avdallah tells them where Abu Ahmad is hiding. Nurit cannot watch any longer. Avihai joins her outside after having bandaged the sheikh's broken hands. She asks him how they can possibly torture an old man, and he replies that they are like fight dogs, they pounce. Does he ever think of his son? Avihai replies: "We were trained not to think. You know why? Because if I stop, to think about him for just a split second, I'll become petrified with fear. I won't be able to move." Nurit: "I don't want this to happen to me. It's like being dead." Avihai: "Then you don't belong here. You are putting us at risk."[13]

Avihai is, of course, right. He is the team's sniper, protecting them from above when they are in an operation. I understand his reasoning. Given the team's tasks, they must rely on each other, because every second can mean being shot or make it home alive. The team simply cannot afford the luxury of second thoughts or regrets, let alone moral musings. They are like the fingers of a hand, fully operative only together.

How they come to terms with their activities after an operation, is, however, a different issue; all of them are suffering of post-traumatic stress disorder, bouts of depression and have difficult relations with their wives and children. Most of them self-medicate with vodka, whisky, and cigarettes; some of them, especially the older members, sometimes express their wish to leave and return to a peaceful, civilian life, but their sense of duty is stronger. This loyalty is the basis of the team.

Walid, Shirin's cousin and an admirer of Abu Ahmad, has pressed Defence Minister Avitai into composing a list of 50 Hamas prisoners whom he wants to be released in a prisoner swap in exchange for Boaz. This is Hamas' principal advantage over Shin Bet: its members are not afraid to die, always ready to sacrifice themselves and others, to become shahids, Muslim martyrs. Amir/Doron visits Shirin, who tells him that Walid forced her to plant a device in Boaz stomach; she did not remove a kidney, as Hamas has claimed in an

---

[13] S1:E7.

earlier media release. Abu Ahmad now wants Gideon Avitai instead of the 50 Hamas prisoners. To parade the Israeli defence minister through Ramallah's streets and then execute him in public would be a smashing success for Hamas. Time is of the essence, and Doron and his team are prepared: prisoner swap yes, but with a surprise.

Nurit abducts Abu Ahmad's daughter Abir from a shop. Walid is increasingly suspicious of Abu Ahmad's motives, thinking of his own promotion in Hamas. Abu Samara, an elderly Hamas leader, tells Walid that once the panther is finally in paradise, he would use his influence to promote Walid to Hamas wing commander. The panther aka radical Abu Ahmad with his Sarin bombs has become a nuisance and burden for Hamas, an organisation that is not exactly known for its willingness to find a compromise with the Israelis.

When the team meets Walid and his men in a wadi, the scene reminded me immediately of the most famous duel in film: High Noon, the duel of good versus evil. Walid's men push Boaz out of the car; he is stumbling towards the team, hoping to go home. On the other side, some 100m away, the team, clad in Palestinian scarfs, pulls Sheikh Avdallah and the little girl out of their car—and we see Doron's blue eyes, full of hatred. Little Abir and the sheikh are wearing explosive belts, very visible to Walid and his men. Doron is one step ahead, putting Abu Ahmad under enormous psychological pressure: if he explodes Boaz, Doron will explode the sheikh and daughter Abir. He thus tops Abu Ahmad's threat. Was Abu Ahmad a reasonable person, he would understand that he cannot kill Boaz, since doing so would prompt the Israelis to blow up the sheikh and his daughter. Yet, he is a radical, caught in an emotional haze of hatred and revenge, willing to sacrifice his own child for his plans. He commands Walid to explode Boaz, and, seeing Boaz die, Doron explodes the sheikh. Little Abir is hurt by splinters of the sheikh's belt. Then, Doron is wandering around, in a state of shock and pain after having seen his brother-in-law blown to pieces. He sleeps over in a mosque, where kind Palestinian men take care of him. Driven by his instinct for shelter and safety, he goes to Shirin. After the battle, the wounded male seeks the comfort, kindness, and care of the female who is in his thoughts and heart. Shirin dresses his wounds. They spend the night together.

Since Moreno obviously has no control over his team, Defence Minister Avitai fires him, and Moreno gets drunk in his office. We see the lousy little fridge, where he keeps his drinks. The next day, Moreno goes to Avitai's office and blackmails him: Israel's press would have a field day reporting that the minister and Moreno had shot five Palestinians when they served together in the IDF years ago. This killing qualifies as war crime, and the minister, a self-interested career politician, has no choice: he withdraws Moreno's notice.

In the meantime, we see Gabi, again using his psychological skills to convince Nassrin to emigrate to Germany. He has driven her to Hadassah hospital, where the best eye surgeon has operated on little Abir. "Let's play pretend", Gabi says to Nassrin, "let's pretend that your husband is actually dead. You could leave without him. You and your children could be off to Berlin, a new beginning, no Jews, no Arabs, no war." Nassrin: "Suppose I'm interested, what must I do to make it happen?" "Help me catch his ghost."[14] This is a most convincing offer: at no point in time, Hamas members can accuse Nassrin of collaboration, as she and Captain Ayub spoke hypothetically. How can you help catch a ghost? A ghost is not real, and everybody 'knows' that the panther is dead. Gabi thus opens mental doors to Nassrin she did not know existed.

Gabi, father of five children and ex-husband to three ex-wives, tells Nassrin that he misses a wife to come home to in the evenings—and the viewer is puzzled: has Gabi just offered marriage to Nassrin? I first thought yes, but then, after replaying this scene twice, I changed my mind. Palestinian women are not free; they are subjects to their fathers, brothers, cousins, and husbands. Even a top-educated medical doctor like Shirin must wear a headscarf while at work and in public. Such are the social conventions made by men. I think this insinuation of Gabi's, politely, softly, and respectfully presented to Nassrin, is a psychological trick to make her feel comfortable, to boost her confidence as an Arab woman, who dares to think the unthinkable: to leave her husband. Hey, if even Captain Ayub, the almighty commanding officer of Shin Bet, our arch enemy, finds me attractive, my life as a woman is not over. I have a future. I can do it, I can leave, and my children shall grow up in peace in Berlin, where I grew up. My daughter won't have to wear a head scarf, marry young and bear children; she will be free to choose what to do with her life. She will have a better life than me, and my boy will not be

---

[14] S1:E9.

pressed into joining Hamas. He can study, choose the life he wants to have. Both my children shall be free and, one day, so God will, I shall have grandchildren.

Gabi's move is superb psychology, or rather, excellent psychological warfare, since it targets three goals: first, his offer of marriage of which he knows that Nassrin must reject it reinforces Nassrin's decision to emigrate. Second, Nassrin leaving with the children, will, in turn, put Abu Ahmad under pressure. To the Hamas members and their families, he is a loser, a man who has lost control over his wife and children. Oh look, people in the West Bank will say, the panther, officially dead, is here in hiding, but I have heard that the wife and kids are in Germany. Nassrin has left him, she doesn't respect him anymore, so why should we? The reputation of a Hamas member is, literally, his life; if I lose my reputation, and people think I am a traitor or collaborator, I am as good as dead.[15] Third, Abu Ahmad's loss of face plays right into the hands of the Hamas leadership, strengthening Abu Samara's position to, once and for all, get rid of that loose cannon with his Sarin bombs.

---

[15] The practice of declaring a person a traitor or collaborator equals a death penalty: this person is no longer subject to the law, and everybody can kill him or her. In Christian medieval times, this practice was referred to as being declared 'vogelfrei'; the moment the king, duke or emperor has declared me 'vogelfrei', everybody can kill me, as I am, literally, free as a bird. But I am also vulnerable as a bird, and everybody can shoot down a bird. Once you are dead, you won't receive a Christian burial. Birds can feed of your corpse. See https://www.bpb.de/kurz-knapp/lexika/das-junge-politik-lexikon/321350/vogelfrei/ accessed 9 October 2023.

As she is hunted by Hamas, Doron hides Shirin in a hotel, but the concierge recognizes her and calls Walid: his cousin has just gone up to a room with an unknown man. This is, according to the cultural codex of the Palestinians, outrageous behaviour, and Shirin would be killed, if it were not for Walid, who is in love with her and offers her marriage to save her. Furthermore, Abu Ahmad has told Walid in no uncertain terms that Shirin deserves to die, because an unknown man had killed his two fighters whom he had sent to arrest her. In Abu Ahmad and Hamas' eyes, Shirin is a traitor and a whore because she has gone to a hotel with a man who is not her husband.

HQ and Doron make a next move: he volunteers as a suicide bomber, hoping to meet Abu Ahmad, who is known for always meeting his suicide bombers in person before their mission. Abu Ahmad's people are working on his suicide belt, but when a Hamas member asks Doron to give him all his earthly belongings, Moreno's HQ loses the listening device planted in Doron's packet of cigarettes. In the meantime, Walid inquires at the HQ of the Palestinian Authority about a certain Amir, member of the Palestinian Preventive Security. Gabi's friend Abu Maher is the head of the Authority, and because of his willingness to negotiate with the Israelis, Hamas considers him a traitor. The officers at the Palestinian HQ are bursting of laughter and show Walid a clip: no other than Captain Ayub has visited the alleged Palestinian operative Amir in prison—which makes Amir a traitor and collaborator, or then Amir is Shin Bet.

This information strengthens Walid's position: he calls Abu Ahmad's people who are preparing Doron for his suicide mission. Doron is exposed, but the team barges in and saves him, shooting everybody. *Fauda* series 1 ends with Walid visiting his once admired leader Abu Ahmad in his hiding place. Motivated by his love for Shirin, to save her life, and, also driven by his ambition to become a Hamas leader, Walid shoots the panther in the head, from behind, Soviet execution style. Doron and Shirin have a date at the *Café au lait*, when she receives a text from Walid with the clip showing Gabi and Doron. She is hurt because Amir has lied to her. In a Tel Aviv hotel, Nassrin learns from Gabi that the panther is dead; she leaves with her children for Berlin.

S2:E1 introduces the series' villain, Abu Nidal, aka Nidal al-Makdasi, portrayed by Firas Nassar.[16] Nidal is the oldest son of Sheikh Avdallah, whom Doron had exploded in series 1. Nidal returns from Syria to the West Bank to revenge his father's death. From a conversation with his little brother Samir who lives with pregnant wife Marwa at his mother's house, we learn that Nidal has had difficult years behind him, doing drugs in Amsterdam before he found God. Nidal is more radical than Abu Ahmad since Isis has sent him to promote its ideology in the West Bank. This means to dress captured persons in US-prison style orange jumpsuits, position them in front of a camera, and have them read an

---

[16] At the time of writing, on 7 October 2023, Hamas has attacked the South of Israel from Gaza, murdering Israeli civilians in several kibbutzim. They have abducted young people who visited the Nova music festival in Southern Israel and Jewish families from their homes. The video clips Hamas has uploaded are terrifying, especially those who show abducted young women and children. The IDF is retaliating with massive bombing of Gaza. The death toll in Israel is 200 persons, rising.

Isis pamphlet that accuses the satanic West. Isis fighters wear black balaclavas and cut the victim's throat with a knife or a machete, then post the clip on social media and spread it to news channels. To Hamas, Isis is a dangerous competition in the terror business.

We see Nidal in a car with Walid and another man. They are looking at a bus stop, where civilians and IDF soldiers are waiting. Nidal speaks Hebrew and can pass the border checkpoints anytime. He instructs the third man: deposit the bag at the bus station and return immediately to the car. The man trusts Nidal, places the bag—and Nidal pushes the button. The man is blown to pieces like the Israeli citizens waiting for the bus. Nidal has no problem at all to kill people, even persons who trust and admire him.

Doron and his father Amos Kavilio visit a Bedouin tribe; the sheikh is Amos' friend, and they do business together. The Bedouins are Israeli citizens and Muslims, and Amos is an Arab Jew. Their friendship demonstrates that one can live in peace together by respecting the other's faith and way of life. On their way back home to Amos' farm, a gunman attacks Doron and Amos. Walid visits Shirin in her apartment; he has to disguise himself since the IDF is watching Shirin's house. From a picture in a frame placed in her apartment we learn that they are married. Walid wants to have a baby with Shirin, and if the saying that love makes blind is true, then Walid is blind in his feelings for Shirin. She is grateful to him, which is not the same as love. It is visible in her face that she is walking a fine line with Walid; she married him to save herself and her mother.

The Bedouin sheikh lets Doron know that he should visit them. When Doron arrives, the sheikh shows him a young man they have caught; the drug addict admitted to the Bedouins that Sheikh Avdallah's son paid him to kill Amos and Doron. Moreno and the team interpret the attack on Doron's father as personal mission to revenge his father.

Um Nidal, the widow of Sheikh Avdallah, warns her elder son Nidal not to take revenge. She wants the violence to stop, and her younger son Samir should not get involved. Nidal promises nothing, although he clearly loves his mother. He rents a room at the back of a Nablus barber shop where he meets his young followers. The six Palestinian young men are studying Hebrew at Israeli universities. They are Jewish impostors, wearing the Jewish kippa and looking like Israeli students. Because they speak Hebrew, they can pass the border checkpoints into Israel and return to the West Bank. One of the young Palestinians is Abu Maher's son. Nidal is radicalizing the young men by evoking their sense of self-importance. He treats them respectfully as long as they obey his Isis creed. His saying "We come before family and everything else"[17] seems to promise them an attractive future in a group that is better than Hamas, where they would have to climb the hierarchy. With Nidal, their youth is no hindrance for great tasks. Because Nidal apparently takes them seriously, they admire him, trusting him blindly.

Moreno's unit has a new member: Sagi, played by Idan Amedi, takes an instant shine to Nurit. The boys call her 'Chuck Nurit', comparing her to Chuck Norris because of her

---

[17] S2:E4.

martial arts talent. Nurit, however, is in love with Moreno, their commander-in-chief; they have to keep their relationship a secret. Intel tells the team that Nidal is going to meet somebody at the mosque in Nablus. The team is in position, yet Nidal fires a rocket into a café close to the mosque, and then escapes on a motorcycle. The team chases him in a car, and when Moreno learns that Nidal is driving towards the location where Shin Bet has set up its command post for the operation, he jumps into a jeep with a soldier, joining in the hunt from the opposite side. One thinks that Nidal cannot escape, being caught between the team and Moreno closing in on him, but Nidal is not stupid. He has anticipated being chased. When Moreno and the soldier are but 50m away from him, Nidal explodes a bomb he has placed earlier in the narrow street. Moreno and his soldier die.[18]

Abu Samara talks to Walid: he wants to meet this al-Makdasi, a new troublemaker for Hamas. When he meets Nidal in a Catholic Church, greeted personally by the priest, he tells Nidal he should obey the Hamas high command. Nidal has only contempt for Abu Samara: the last fighter who did something significant for the movement had been the panther. No one tells him to renounce on his personal revenge, to revenge his father Sheikh Avdallah.[19] Nidal is more dangerous than the panther, because he is single, follows Isis ideology, reports to his masters in Syria and has nothing to lose. The panther Abu Ahmad had had to hide for

---

[18] S2:E1.
[19] S2:E2.

years, putting wife Nassrin and the children under pressure, and the family was his weak point. Nidal, on the other hand, is not burdened with a wife and children; the only family he cares for is his mother and his little brother Samir with wife Marwa.

Doron and Steve arrive together at the Moreno family's house to pay their respects. Steve meets Anat, Moreno's beautiful young sister, and they fall for each other. The team is sitting in the garden, sharing their memories of their commander-in-chief. When somebody mentions Moreno's dysfunctional fridge, the tipsy team raids his office, gets the fridge, and places it in a safe space in the countryside. In a symbolic act, remembering their commander, they shoot at the fridge. Their new commander is Eli, called back from a training stay in England.

Eli senses that the team is not as united in its resolve as it should be: personal animosities are destroying trust. He organizes a training session of boxing and close combat, and this psychological experiment tells him what he wants to know. He has Doron fight Naor, and Nurit Sagi. Doron and Naor have feelings of hatred of each other because of Naor's former relationship with Doron's ex-wife Gali, while Nurit, pained by grief for the loss of Moreno, goes against new team member Sagi with a vengeance.

To get at Nidal, the team abducts Samir, Nidal's younger brother. Naor leaves the team because he objects Doron's beating up the young man after they have abducted him from a doctor's practice he has visited with pregnant Marwa. From Doron's perspective, Samir is the little brother of the man who wanted to kill his father. He must know something.

Family always knows something. When Gabi walks into the interrogation room, he thinks shaken Samir is an easy prey; Gabi is aware that by sending Marwa a picture of Samir's bloody face he increases Nidal's hatred and resolve; he wants to flush him out. Nidal knows that Hamas has an IT specialist who can find out where Doron Kavilio lives. He pressures him into looking up Doron's address.

Doron puts a camera in Shirin's apartment, hiding it in the backside of her marriage photo; he uses the few minutes to tell Shirin that there is a way out for her and gives her an email address. If she wants out, she can contact him. Posing as businessman Fadi, Nidal rents the lower apartment in a house owned by wealthy widow Hanan. Hanan is a Palestinian woman who regrets the radicalisation Hamas has brought about the people in the West Bank; she misses the old times when she and her husband had Israeli friends. Friends visit each other, knowing that they are safe.

When Gabi, with the help of astute young officer Dana, played by Meirav Shirom, finds out that Abu Maher's son is on the list of Palestinian students who are studying Hebrew,[20] he warns his friend. Abu Maher, a loving father, is suspicious of his son, but believes his lies. By employing Maher jun. at his office at the Palestinian Authority, he thinks he has him under control. Nidal gives Maher jun. an ashtray with a listening device to know what the Authority is talking about. Nidal can use this information against the Hamas leadership, especially Abu Samara. Since Abu Karim, Hamas's

---

[20] S2:E4.

financial officer, refuses to give Nidal money, he and his student-boys raid the office at night and steal Hamas' funds.

Nidal stands in front of Doron's house and talks to son Ido; Gabi has Doron's family moved into a safe house. Shirin, shocked by the lyrics of a Hamas song sung to her by the little daughter of an acquaintance,[21] decides to leave the West Bank for good. She wants to return to France with her mother. When Gabi interrogated her a few weeks ago, he offered to have her and her mother flown out, in exchange for Walid.[22] Shirin sends Doron an email. They meet at the rooftop at the hospital, and he gives her a new passport and a new SIM card for secure communication. She wants Walid imprisoned and not killed. The meeting point for her extraction is the hotel Four Seasons in Ramallah.

In front of the Four Seasons, Shirin gets into the car to be driven to Israel; Walid and his boys stop the car, slip in, and he threatens her with a gun. How does he know that she wants to flee? A nurse paid by Nidal has seen Shirin going up to the rooftop a few days ago; she informed Nidal,[23] who then told Walid that his wife is up to something. Here, I wondered: has Nidal deliberately set up Walid to be caught by the Israelis, to get rid of him? Walid in an Israeli prison would be a blow to Hamas. Nidal's main goal is to replace Hamas with Isis, to make Isis the principal political factor in the West Bank and the Gaza strip. Gone the PLO with Arafat, that joke of a Palestinian leader and weakling. Gone Hamas,

---

[21] S2:E4. The song praises Hamas members' martyrdom and the honour to die for the movement.
[22] S2:E2.
[23] S2:E5.

those cowards, who always hide in their stupid tunnels. Gone lazy Hezbollah in Lebanon, whose leaders are more interested in gambling and drinking in Qatar casinos than fighting the Zionists here and now. The future is with Isis—or so Nidal must think.

One of Walid's boys searches Shirin's handbag and finds her new passport. Shirin does not know that Gabi has planted a chip in the passport's backside. Walid's lackey destroys Shirin's pass before a police car stops them. The Palestinian police officers are Steve and Sagi in disguise, and their task is to free Shirin. Sagi and Steve shoot both bodyguards, then Doron arrives and arrests Walid. The team returns to HQ and celebrates its success, toasting to Boaz. They never forget their loved ones. Doron brings Shirin to a safe house, where she has to wait until she can fly out. It is sparse there, and Doron decides to take her to his father's farm. He senses that she is upset by her betrayal of Walid who saved her life by marrying her.

Dana interrogates Walid, who is tougher than the team and Gabi thought. They put Naor into Walid's prison cell, expecting that Naor can get information from Walid.[24] Yet Walid sees through Naor who is playing a Palestinian; he identifies him after a couple of days as impostor and spy. This method of information-gathering has catastrophically failed, due to Walid's high IQ and his loyalty to Hamas. As good as Naor's Arabic is, he slipped with one word, and Walid immediately knew that Naor is an impostor.

---

[24] S2:E7.

Late at night, Doron and Shirin arrive at Amos' farm. His father senses that Shirin is more to Doron than a recruited asset he needs to protect. "Doron, no good can come of this." "I know."[25] Amos is a kind host; he cooks breakfast for Shirin the next morning, and they have a nice conversation, much as if they were in a Paris bistro for a harmless Sunday lunch.

The team abducts Abu Samara when he leaves the house of his lover early in the morning; they bring him to a spot in the countryside, where Gabi is sitting on a camping chair, cooking coffee. Abu Samara apparently knows nothing about that al-Makdasi, but Gabi is in the stronger position: he shows him pictures on his smart phone that display the Hamas leader with his mistress *in flagrante delicto*. Particularly juicy is the fact that Abu Samara's lover is the widow of a Hamas fighter who has fallen for the movement. Gabi tells him that he has been receiving these pictures every Tuesday morning. Gabi is ruthless: I have information that can destroy you. If I publish this information, your reputation will be finished, but not only your reputation, your life. In Hamas' moral codex, sleeping with the widow of a fighter who has lost his life for the movement would be considered a deadly sin. Abu Samara and his lover would die.

One must acknowledge Abu Samara's clear thinking and instinct for survival. He knows when he has lost. To protect himself and his lover, he agrees to Gabi's plan: to replace Walid, who is in Israeli custody, with Nidal, to flush him out. In the meantime, Dana tries to break Walid, showing him a photo of Shirin holding hands with Doron. When Gabi enters

---

[25] S2:E6.

the interrogation room, he asks Walid if he knows that Shirin is pregnant? This is the crack to Walid's mind, to break him, to make him tell them where Nidal is hiding. "Want to see the test results? Who will raise your kid now?"[26] Walid is shaken, and Gabi, with his soft voice, whispering in Arabic, goes for his jugular: "We can treat you like a king in prison. Even God won't know you helped us." This ensures Walid that once he is released from prison, nobody can accuse him of having collaborated with the Israelis. If not even God knows, who could possibly know?

HQ informs Doron that Shirin's time to leave for France is now. The lovers have spent two days of bliss and peace together on Amos' farm, and they are planning their future. Doron promises that he shall visit her in Paris. When Amos says good-bye to Doron, he embraces his son. We see Doron's face; he is surprised by that hug. Doron and Shirin have last minutes together in a café, and he gives her a necklace, a token of his love. Then, Doron gets a phone call from the team. He and Shirin rush back to Amos' farm. Too late. Nidal has cut Amos' throat in Isis style, filmed it, and put it on social media.[27] The team is there. Doron is out of his mind; the pain to see his dad's body being taken away, is, to me, the key scene in *Fauda*, the very reason why I think that there will never be peace in the Middle East, only a continuous state of alert and, at the best, a stable ceasefire. Why?

---

[26] S2:E8.
[27] S2:E8.

Smoking a cigarette in front of his father's house, grieving Doron is thinking, and the only rational conclusion to the riddle how Nidal knew the address of Amos' farm is Shirin. The second he learns of his dad's murder his mistrust of Shirin is born because of the simple fact that she is not a Jew. He walks up to her, shouting: "What have you done? Who did you talk to? You tipped them off, didn't you? Take her in, she is an informer, she brought them here."[28]

This principal lack of trust is inherited from fathers and mothers' experiences, on both sides. Not even the love of Doron and Shirin can be a new beginning; too painful are the memories and the hurt on both sides. There is no hour zero, no fresh beginning, because that would mean to forgive and move on, which is very easy for us to say. We do not live in Israel, and we do not have this experience of daily threat.

Shirin is innocent, but nobody knows that; following Doron's accusation, Shirin is arrested. In the interrogation room, Dana accuses her of being a terrorist. This has implications; she could end up with a long prison sentence. When Walid is brought into the interrogation room and placed opposite his wife, he spots the necklace—and loses it: "You have nowhere to go, you traitor!"[29] This is a death sentence, and Shirin knows what awaits her. If she gets a ten-year prison sentence, she will be released in her mid-forties; can she then go back home to Nablus? Will her mother still be alive? Would she be safe there, condemned by her husband as traitor?

---

[28] S2:E9.
[29] S2:E9.

Amos' murder has affected the team; if not even an old man is safe on his desert farm with his horses and sheep, who is safe? Anat visits Steve, who sleeps with his gun: "Do you realize how insane it is for a person to be scared to death inside his own home?"[30] Young and naïve Anat, who should know better as the sister of a Shin Bet commander killed in action, wants to leave, like Gali. The women see only one solution: to leave Israel with their men. But their men don't want to leave; they want to carry on, protect Israel, which is not only their state, but also, in an extended view and feeling, their family home.

So far, HQ has not been successful in breaking Walid, but Naor, wanting to reconcile with Doron, has a plan: abduct Walid and make him talk. Again, this is an operation Gabi knows nothing about—or pretends not to know. Gabi and Doron are close because both have a pragmatic view and approach to operations. If they ignore the law to protect the state, that's what they do. The team abducts Walid when he is being transferred to another prison; they pose as a medical team and bring Walid to the Bedouin sheikh's village. The Bedouin sheikh and his men had visited Doron to pay their respects to Amos. Friendship has nothing to do with faith; friendship is based on respect and tolerance, the principal view that we are all human beings.

Arrogant and highly intelligent Walid thinks that he can manipulate the team, but when Doron shoots a bullet into his leg, the pain is excruciating. Walid talks, telling the team about the Nablus barber shop. Walid tries to manipulate

---

[30] S2:E9.

Nurit, begging her to help him, appealing to her female instincts. In Walid's mind and cultural codex, females are servants and 2nd class citizens; they must obey men, even if they are total strangers. Any man can command any woman, in his view. With blank eyes, Nurit looks at him, turns around, grabs a gallon of fuel and pours the fuel over Walid. Doron threatens him with a lighter, but does not set him on fire, because he has promised Shirin to let him live. His words are his bound. We see Naor shooting Walid in the head. Naor is not bound by any promise, and killing Walid is a sign of respect to Doron. Doron and Naor have rekindled their friendship. Two little boys find Walid's body in the countryside, clad into a white blanket with the Arabic word 'traitor' on it.

Gabi talks to Shirin and believes her; she knows nothing about Amos' murder. But he also tells her that her leave for Paris has been postponed. It is not yet sure that she can leave, but she is released from prison. Gabi brings her to the safe house where she has been before. Doron, who has come to his senses after having talked to Gabi, goes to the safe house to apologize to Shirin. He finds her in the bathroom; she has hanged herself. From Shirin's point of view, suicide is the last act of rational self-determination, born of desperation. She has, indeed, nowhere to go; Doron, whom she loves, is her enemy now; her leave for France is not sure; her mother's life is threatened because of her betrayal of Walid, and once released from prison, Hamas would kill her and her mother, her family's name shamed as traitors for eternity. Shirin's suicide deeply affects Doron; he falls into a depression, and only Eli can convince him to come back.[31] They have to eliminate Nidal, and the team needs him.

The team's plan for the operation at the Nablus barber shop stands: the plan is to catch Nidal when he meets his followers-students. Samir, Nidal's younger brother, is there when the team throws a grenade into the shop. Steve gets hit, while Doron catches Samir, shouting to Nidal that he has his brother. Nidal does not give up, keeps shooting at the team, and when Doron pushes Samir into the firing line, Samir dies from the bullets of his brother. Had Nidal given up, his brother would be alive, but not even Doron's warning makes him stop. Who is responsible for Samir's death? Doron who pushes the young man into the firing line, knowing that he will die, or Nidal, who has been warned, but keeps shooting? This is a difficult moral question, and I cannot answer it. At the end of the day, every operation is about the survival of the state. Nidal flees.

Pregnant Marwa, Samir's wife, hears on loudspeakers that Samir has fallen, a shahid for the movement. In the meantime, Gabi takes care of Maher jun.; because he is a friend of Abu Maher, his son gets preferential treatment. Gabi sends him to Jordan; from there, junior will be sent to Denmark. Gabi could have junior imprisoned in Israel for his cooperation with Nidal, but he values his friendship to Abu Maher, one of the few Palestinians who is not radicalized by hatred. Abu Maher once tried to convince his son that a peaceful co-existence with Israel would be to the benefit of the Palestinians: he took him to lunch in Tel Aviv, showing

---

[31] S2:E10.

him the city's prosperity and wealth. But junior was too radicalized by Nidal to understand what his father was trying to tell him.

Nidal sends Marwa a note; he wants to see her. She is the widow of his little brother, and the few things I know about the Muslim cultural codex is that the brother has to take care of the widow of his brother by marrying her. Nidal is charming, friendly, and has been coveting young Marwa for a long time; he tells her about how they grew up together, reminding her of their childhood. She was such a beautiful little girl. He offers her marriage. Marwa and her mother-in-law blame Nidal for Samir's death, and the young woman spits into his face.[32]

Doron drives son Ido to a Judo tournament; his car is hit by a truck. When Doron wakes up, he is clad in a US style orange prison suit and chained to a chair—at the mercy of Nidal. Doron's son Ido is also a captive of Nidal. What then happens is one of the most touching screenwriting I have seen. Nidal forces Doron to say good-bye to his son, and wants him to read some Isis message, while filming him.

Gabi interrogates Marwa "You either tell me where al-Makdasi is hiding, or I'll make you have a miscarriage. I'll do it."[33] Marwa, in fear for her baby, gives him a paper slip Nidal gave her. Gabi gives Abu Samara instructions. The team drives close to the compound and spots a little boy; Nidal uses little Ismail to bring them food and water. The team

---

[32] S2:E11.
[33] S2:E12.

catches the frightened little boy and promises him not to tell his father. Nidal and Hamas use male children as couriers.

Doron and Nidal talk. We see how much Nidal enjoys seeing his enemy humiliated and at his mercy. Doron is quite certain that he is going to die, but wanting to save his son, he talks to Nidal. Nidal: "You killed my father. I killed your father." Doron: "But remember, I am not like you. I don't kill civilians; I don't murder children."[34] Nidal tells his lackey to get the camera. Doron hugs Ido for a last time, whispering into his ears that if there is soon some shooting, Ido should lay low. Doron has to kneel in front of the camera but gets up, refusing to read the Isis text.

Suddenly, Abu Samara and his men are barging in. They shoot Nidal and his bodyguard. Gabi blackmailing Abu Samara has saved Doron and Ido's lives. Nidal is wounded but chases Abu Samara, and Doron, who is also hurt, grabs the gun of the dead man and chases after Nidal. He finds him lying in a room, looking at Ido who is standing in front of him, pointing a gun at him. Doron implores his little boy to put the gun down. Ido obeys, finally. Abu Nidal grins at Doron; he knows that he is going to die in minutes, but in his way of thinking, he has won. Why? He thinks he has planted Isis ideology in the West Bank, that his student-followers are going to carry on his mission. The team arrives and brings Doron and Ido home.

---

[34] S2:E12.

II b. The Abduction of Captain Ayub, *Fauda* series 4

The plot of series 4 centres on Gabi, aka Captain Ayub. In series 3, Abu Maher died in a Hamas attack launched to prevent him signing a cooperation deal with Gabi. Avihai, the team's sniper, shot an IDF soldier; in the heat of the battle, he had made a wrong decision. Avihai was shot in the stomach, and a kind Palestinian taxi driver called a Palestinian doctor who could not help Doron and Avihai. There are decent people everywhere. Doron was about to bring Avihai to a hospital which would have prompted his arrest by Hamas, but Nurit and Steve saved them in the last minute with their ambulance. Avihai died. At the end of series 3, Hamas pressed a medical aid who was taking care of Gabi's physiotherapy into a scheme to kill him, but the team diverted the plan. Nurit finally understood that she and Sagi belong together and moved in with him. Doron had not been in contact with the team for one and a half years, due to a fall out with Eli who had no choice than to suspend him because of the circumstances of Avihai's death. Doron's children are studying in Boston. Abu Osama has replaced Abu Maher as the head of the Palestinian Authority.

Series 4 is set in Hebron in the southern West Bank, and the terror group the team fights is the Shiite Hezbollah that operates at the Lebanese Israeli border. Gabi has been promoted to the head of the international branch, with Dana and Raphael replacing him at HQ. Dana gets information from Abu Osama that there is something brewing in Molenbeek in Belgium. Doron shows up at Nurit and Sagi's wedding, and everybody is happy to see him. Omar Tawalbe, played by Amir Boutrous, is Gabi's mole in Molenbeek; when he calls Gabi he is in panic, telling Gabi that he thinks that the members of his Belgian Hezbollah cell are suspecting him of working for Shin Bet. Gabi promises to come to see him, as Omar is like a son to him. He wants Doron to be his bodyguard in Belgium.

At night, Gabi, Doron and two security officers drive to the meeting point when Omar calls: the location has changed. This is a big mistake of Gabi's: the informer never determines the meeting point. Gabi should have followed the security protocol, postponed the meeting, and suggested a new location, but he feels safe and ignores Doron's protest. Is Gabi arrogant or too trusting? Why does he ignore the security protocol? They meet Omar in an apartment on the second floor of a house with a large courtyard and several entry points. Doron is immediately suspicious and checks the courtyard. When he is back up at the apartment, he finds both security guards shot. Omar and Gabi are gone.[35]

Police officer Maya Benjamin, portrayed by Lucy Ayoub, is back home from an undercover mission; she is a member of the Tel Aviv police drug squad and married to an Israeli police officer. Maya is an Israeli citizen of Palestinian origin; she is the sister of Omar. Since Dana has information that Omar is a Hezbollah member, Shin Bet arrests Maya and her family. She has not seen him for four years. Radical Adel Tawalbe is Omar and Maya's cousin and a terror king pin in the Jenin refugee camp. He is preparing rockets to fire them into Israel. The team travels to Belgium to find Gabi.

---

[35] S4:E1.

Omar is torturing Gabi. The physical pain is too much: Gabi gives Omar the names of his Palestinian informers in Jenin and Hebron. They all die. Why has Omar betrayed Gabi? Omar: "My dear Gabi, you have turned us all into traitors and now you'll be turning us into Palestine's heroes."[36] The team raids a Molenbeek's mosque and abducts the Imam. In the woods, he tells them that Ibrahim, one of his faithful, is seeing a young woman named Nassrin. With the help of intelligence from HQ, the team finds Nassrin. Threatened by Nurit, the young woman who has just got infusions and IV bags from a pharmacy, tells her where she has to deliver the medical goods to: a quarter in Molenbeek. The team inspects the quarter, and Nurit finds out in a friendly chat with a Muslim mother that thugs have taken over one house.

Raphael, the team's new commander-in-chief, calls Angela, the head of Belgian counterterrorism, asking her for support. Studying the plan of the quarter, she finds a tunnel that connects two houses. The team is frantically searching the house where they think Gabi is being kept. Nurit gets shot in the leg. She is pregnant but hasn't told Sagi yet. A Belgian Swat team member finds the tunnel, and they raid the other house. Gabi hears the team calling his name in Hebrew, stabs one of his torturers and gets shot. He loses a lot of blood.

When a spy drone delivers footage of a coffin being unloaded from a plane at Beirut airport, the team, back in Tel Aviv, thinks that Gabi is dead. A rabbi is there, for psychological-religious comfort. Doron is the only one who

---

[36] S4:E2.

asks the principal question: "Have you seen the body?"[37] The amount of blood the forensic examiners have found in the Molenbeek apartment makes Gabi's survival unlikely. Even Gabi's son Itamar has come to terms with the loss of his father. Maya receives an encrypted video message from Omar. He wants her to get something from their mother's house. Dana tells Doron that Shani Russo is back; she is replacing Nurit who is in hospital. Russo, portrayed by Inbar Lavi, is as tough as Nurit and she likes Doron, who is like an older brother to her. Eli, who is in a relationship with Magith, Avihai's widow, thinks about his future; he wants to leave the team. Dana: "I need you, we're in the midst of a war –" Eli: "We're always in the midst of a war. Question is, when is there a ceasefire?" Dana: "Never, and you know it."[38]

Hezbollah terrorists kill Kaspi and Lavi; tortured Gabi has revealed to Omar where they live. Doron and Dana are attacked in their homes; the service gets the families to a safe house. Maya finds the packet from her mother's house in Jenin—passports for Omar and wife Aisha. The team arrests Musab, the former driver of Abu Osama, who has joined Adel's terror group. He wants to protect his lover, Jenin pharmacist Ismail. Blackmailed by HQ, Musab is collaborating. According to Hezbollah's moral codex, being gay is a death sentence. Elderly baker Khaled from Jenin who has lost his only son to a Hezbollah operation tells Dana that Adel and his men meet regularly at a garage.[39]

---

[37] S4:E4.
[38] S4:E4.
[39] S4:E8.

Omar calls sister Maya, instructing her to meet a colleague of his at a restaurant in the Golan Heights. Doron introduces himself as Salah, later revealing himself to Maya as his Palestinian alter ego, Amir Mahajne. In the meantime, Eli, Sagi, Russo and Steve observe Adel's house in Jenin, where wife Shara and son Kareem live. Doron and Maya travel to Fnajdek in Lebanon to deliver the passports to Aisha. This is Raphael's plan: Omar's phone call to Maya was an elaborate deep fake, sent from HQ via an encrypted app that displays Omar's AI picture.[40] Naturally, HQ has also placed the two passports in Maya's mother's house. The plan is to get Doron to Fnajdek to kidnap Aisha and thus have leverage over Omar. Raphael needs Maya to accompany Doron to get to Fnajdek. The delivery of the passports to Aisha is an elaborate scheme to make Maya collaborate. Maya and Doron get through the Lebanese border, posing as Syrian refuges Nur and Salim al-Hamis who are looking for their son in Lebanon. The border guards believe them and issue temporary passports.

Sagi, who is not himself after having learnt that Nurit is pregnant and unsure if she wants to keep the baby, is restless. To flush Adel out, he places a bomb under a car in front of Adel's house. Before they can get back to their observation post, the door opens, and little Kareem steps out. Sagi and Eli are shouting at him to go back into the house, but it's too late. The bomb explodes; the boy is hurt and brought to the hospital.[41] Sagi just wanted the car to

---

[40] S4:E5.
[41] S4:E5.

explode to make Adel think his family is in danger; the unfortunate coincidence affects Russo deeply. The next day, she visits the boy and his mother in the hospital.

Abu Kareem is Adel's name as a Hamas fighter. He gets TNT delivered to his lab located under the Jenin garage. When he learns that his boy is hurt, he goes to the hospital with Musab and two bodyguards. Adel is not stupid, and neither are his guards. After having shot Kaspi and attacked Dana, Musab has been hiding on Israeli territory and has not been in contact with Adel. Shin Bet blackmailed him with exposing his homosexual relationship with Ismail. Musab has sent Ismail a text that he would not be able to see him for some time. This means that Musab cannot account for some days he had allegedly been in hiding on Israeli territory— which makes Adel and his men suspicious. In the hospital, a bodyguard checks Musab's phone. HQ positions a predator drone over Adel's car once it has his ID confirmed. Adel and Musab drive off, and Musab asks Adel to stop to get cigarettes. Musab is wearing a grey woollen cap. He leaves the car and quickly walks away. The predator launches the rocket, and the car explodes. The team is happy: their spy drone is too far away to show the face: it is Adel who has put on Musab's cap.[42]

Omar is in Beirut with his Hezbollah commander Haj Ali; he has moved up in the ranks because of the abduction of Gabi. Haj Ali, tipped off by an informer, wants to see all papers of the refugees who have passed into Lebanon. His team scrutinizes the pictures and names, and Omar is

---

[42] S4:E6.

shocked to see Maya in disguise. He doesn't know what she is doing in Lebanon. Doron and Maya, under suspicion by the Hezbollah checkpoint guards, kill the two guards and flee with their car and weapons. Now Haj Ali knows that the Syrian refugees are Israeli infiltrators, and Omar tells him that he personally wants to hunt them down.[43]

Doron and Maya hide in the woods; Raphael tells them to reach Tripoli in Lebanon for extraction. He has just aborted the operation; disobeying Raphael's command, Doron and Maya drive to Fnajdek to give Aisha the passports; her house is guarded by Hezbollah fighters. Steve and Russo drive to the garage in Jenin, posing as a Palestinian couple whose car has engine problems. A guy there recognizes Russo from the hospital, and after a shoot-out, the team finds the underground lab with Adel's missiles. He has fled. After a Hezbollah fighter has abducted Maya and Aisha and drives off to bring them to Haj Ali, Doron follows them. He shoots the man and abducts the women to a forest. Maya and Aisha are now his hostages. Maya is shocked by Amir's apparent betrayal, while Aisha is crying all the time. Doron calls Omar and tells him where he can find his sister and wife. Once Omar has given himself up to Doron, he answers the question that has driven Doron all these days: There is no body. Gabi is alive.[44]

Doron has Omar drive them to a Mossad safe house in North Lebanon. There, Omar tells Doron that Haj Ali is keeping Gabi in Beirut and shall deliver him to the Iranians.

---

[43] S4:E7.
[44] S4:E8.

Haj Ali and his men arrive at the heavily guarded compound in the Saifi neighbourhood in Beirut and go down to the basement. Physically, Gabi has recovered from the torture, but he is thinner and seems psychologically broken. He begs Haj not to deliver him to Iran, but Haj orders him to pack his things, once the doctor has confirmed that Gabi is fit to travel. Doron sends Nimer, the head of the safe house, to inspect the neighbourhood, and Nimer takes a pic of Haj when he arrives at the gate, sends it to Doron, and Doron forwards it to HQ. Eli comes up with a plan to free Gabi: with the support of the US Navy Seals, the team will arrive at night in a boat at the coast of Beirut, pose as Lebanese police and free Gabi at one of the border checkpoints where they expect the hand-over to take place.[45] There are three possible border check points: Masnaa, Qualaman and the UN border checkpoint.

Gabi and Haj Ali are driving on the Beirut Damascus highway towards the border to Syria, and Gabi applies his superb psychology, talking for his life, trying to create doubts about Iran in Haj Ali's mind: "You think Iran will save you? Iran? Iran has turned Lebanon into a refugee state. You could have been a thriving country like Israel." Haj Ali: "You mean an occupying country that kills children."[46] The team, clad in Lebanese police uniforms, stops a black van with Haj Ali's right hand, who looks suspiciously at Russo. He gets out of the car and demands to see her ID. Tensions rise and before they are shot by the bodyguards, the team shoots them. Haj

---

[45] S4:E9.
[46] S4:E10.

Ali's right hand refuses to tell them where the handover will take place. Time is of the essence, and Omar, fearing for Maya and Aisha, helps: "Bomb his mother's house in Maroun-al Ras, where his wife and kids are hiding."[47] The right hand of Haj Ali has no choice: he tells the team that Gabi is in the car that is driving to the Qualamun checkpoint.

Haj Ali enjoys talking to Gabi, displaying the psychological thrill of a sadist: "Gabi, someday you'll realize that you'd do the same if you were in my shoes." Gabi: "Tell yourself all the stories you want, sheikh. We're not like you." Ali: "Of course, you're the most moral army in the world." Gabi: "Every day could be your last. You know why they call me Captain Ayoub? Because I'm the curse of anyone who looks at my handsome face." Ali: "Tomorrow, when we hand you over to my Iranian friends, you'll miss me, Captain."[48]

This statement is chilling to the core, and one understands Dana's reasoning. At HQ, she talks to Raphael: "We must consider option B. What he's been through is nothing compared to what lies ahead. Let's spare him the misery."[49] Option B would be to have the car bombed by a drone. Raphael replies that he is not yet done. When Haj Ali and Gabi arrive at the border checkpoint, the team is only minutes away, and HQ must gain time. On the Syrian side, a general and his platoon are waiting. The border gate is open. Before Haj Ali can get Gabi out of the car, the gate is suddenly closing. Gili, one of Raphael's young hackers, has fiddled with

---

[47] S4:E10.
[48] S4:E10.
[49] S4:E10.

the electronics, and it takes some minutes for the border guards to open the gate again—and in this second, the team attacks, shooting at the Syrian platoon and the Lebanese border guards. They all die. Doron rushes to the car, shoots Haj Ali and pulls Gabi out.[50] The team is running towards the extraction point where a chopper is landing. When Gabi spots Omar, he grabs Doron's gun and shoots the young man who has betrayed him.

Maya's interrogation with Dana has come to an end. Dana makes her sign the statement; she is not allowed to speak to anybody about this. Maya is angry and sad, mourning Omar: "Yep, I'm really lucky, you used a police officer, lied to her, fooled her, made her betray her country and risk her life just to wipe out her brother."[51] Maya's complaints seem unfair to me: as an Israeli police officer, she knows the law. The moment she learns about Omar and the passports, she should have refused to play along and withstood Raphael's manipulative plan—which is very easy to say. Had she refused to have anything to do with Omar and ignored the phone call, Raphael would have found another solution to get Doron to Aisha. Yet, because of Maya's respect for her mother, she thought that she should help her brother. What does she mean with betraying her country? She means her ethnic-cultural origins. Maya does not seem to understand that Dana could have brought her to justice in a trial for treason. Maya leaves for Jenin to stay with her

---

[50] S4:E10.
[51] S4:E10.

mother. For the time being, the authorities keep Omar's body, and the family cannot bury him.

In the Jenin hospital, Adel and Shara are looking at their son Kareem. Adel is exhausted, and seeing his ill son, he wants to give up, but Shara implores him: "Stand up to them, be strong. You're the hero of Palestine."[52] Palestinian women are not free, but they are also responsible for inciting and enabling terrorism. Adel wants to stop, but Shara reminds him of his reputation. Here, I wondered: Is Shara willing to sacrifice her son when he is old enough to join Hezbollah? Will Kareem have it easier in Hezbollah if his father has died a shahid's death? Shara seems to be more radical than Adel in her hatred of the Israelis.

Doron takes Gabi to his father's farm, away from the HQ interrogators. Gabi cannot stand being in the house and keeps wandering around; when he falls asleep, he wakes up screaming and crying in pain. His nightmares must be horrible. Doron calls ex-wife Gali, and she manages to convince Gabi that his life is not yet over; everybody is happy that he is back home. They love him. Son Itamar arrives, and they finally hug; this is the beginning of Gabi's healing. Adel, comforted and encouraged by his wife, launches the missiles from Jenin into Israel.

Unlike everybody else, Dana has not been capable of visiting Gabi on Doron's farm. Doron drives Gabi to HQ and tells Dana that Gabi is here. She slips into the car and apologizes. Gabi still suffers from self-reproach, from having talked under torture, but his mind is back to its old self: he

---

[52] S4:E10.

suggests to Dana a plan to eliminate Adel. Release Omar's body and have the family in Jenin give him a proper burial. Why? "Adel is a street kid, he's after respect, wants to be king. He'll never let the PLO or Hamas take credit for his martyr. Once he gets word, he'll gather his men and attend the funeral. You know, they had me read the newspapers there. So I could see what I've done. I wanted to die."[53]

Maya receives a phone call; the Israeli investigation commission has released Omar's body. When Dana tells the team about Gabi's plan to kill Adel at Omar's funeral, Doron is against it because of Maya. He has tender feelings for her. The team goes ahead. Maya and her relatives have received Omar's body and pray for him in a hospital, where the body is going to be prepared for the funeral. Suddenly, four Hamas fighters wearing black balaclavas and green headbands barge in, declaring that Omar is a Hamas martyr and deserves a honourable procession.[54] As Gabi has predicted, Adel rushes to the procession with his men, while the family can do nothing against the Hamas fighters leading the procession and chanting Hamas slogans. Naturally, the procession is shown on local TV.

Then, Doron's feelings and his impulsive character ruin the operation: he pulls Maya away and warns her—go home. She recognizes his eyes and starts to scream, warning the family. Adel and his men escape to the ruin of a building, chased by the team and a platoon of IDF soldiers. A truck blocks the troops sent to reinforce the team, and the heavy

---

[53] S4:E11.
[54] S4:E12.

shooting has its tolls: all IDF soldiers die, and Sagi, Eli and Steve are hit. Russo and Doron chase Adel up the staircase of the house; Russo is hit. While Doron chases Adel, heavily wounded Russo spots Adel's men trying to pull the wounded team members away. She knows what that means: kidnapping Shin Beth soldiers to trade them for a prisoner exchange. Russo screams, warning Doron. He is limping down the staircase, and collapses at the side of Eli, Steve and Sagi. The team members, all shot, lie together, hold hands, and Doron prays.[55] The viewer thinks that they are dying, but then, one hears choppers approaching. They will survive.

Conclusion

Did Kant understand the conditions of war or was he idealistic, believing in the good of mankind? In his times, terrorism of the proportion of today's radical believers did not exist. A handful of West German, French and Italian terrorists of the RAF, Action Directe and the Brigate Rosse terrorized Europe in the 1970s and 1980s. The USA, France and the Russian Federation suffered from Muslim terrorist attacks: 9/11, Charlie Hebdo and the Beslan school killing are sad examples of what radicalized believers do to innocent civilians. Was Kant naïve? Let us look at his principles 1, 5 and 6 he believed would secure a perpetual peace.

Principle 1: "No conclusion of peace shall be considered valid as such if it was made with a secret reservation of the material for a future war." If we put principle 1 on its head, thus a premise *ex negativo*, we find that to keep a war going

---

[55] S4:E12.

on, one must hide one's plans, thus nurture a hidden reservation. In *Fauda*, principle 1 is no guarantee of the survival of the state when in peace negotiations, on the contrary: Shin Bet's task is to protect Israel, and it can realize this protection only by analysing and anticipating the actions of its enemies, that is, by being always on alert. Apart from the various efforts to make peace with the Palestinians,[56] Israel is surrounded by enemies since her foundation. It offered land for peace and did not receive peace.[57] The state cannot afford pacifism; to survive, it must act according to what Kant called *reservatio mentalis*, always being alert and prepared. Anything else would be deliberate suicide.

Furthermore, I doubt that Kant's first principle is applicable to our modern world, since to negotiate a peace agreement means that I must mean it, I must want peace. This requires a lot of trust, but also alertness. It would be dangerously naïve to give up my army once I have signed the peace agreement, since another enemy could attack me. If I am in a stronger position, knowing that I shall win the war, negotiations are not in my best interest. Why negotiate if I am winning? I would give away my advantageous position. If both parties are at a stalemate, the time has come for a ceasefire, which can later become a condition for peace.

Therefore, in our world today, Kant's *reservatio mentalis* is outdated, since no state can afford to completely trust its enemies, not even in peace negotiations. I can negotiate

---

[56] https://www.jewishvirtuallibrary.org/history-and-overview-of-israel-palestinian-negotiations; accessed 20 October 2023.
[57] US economist Thomas Sowell is a superb thinker: https://www.youtube.com/watch?v=aozxj-no98M; accessed 22 October 2023.

peace but that does not mean that I rid myself of my army, leaving my people vulnerable to an attack in the future.

Pacifism is based on the belief that I, demonstrating unconditional (!) trust, am superior: by my sheer moral superiority, I shall convince my enemy to behave as I do, thus, to lay down arms and have a couple of gin tonics and vodkas together. Sure, we all want peace. But what do I do if my principal enemy does not want peace, if his core political identity and final principal moral goal is death, to die for the cause? Pacifism ignores rational thought; it is based on hope, on emotions. My enemy might not share my emotional attitude.

In the real world, and since WWII, if we want to learn from history, pacifism does not work, because the mindset of a radical does not acknowledge self-limitation, only complete victory, absolute domination, the mindset of totalitarianism. Terrorists are absolutists; they do not respect compromise. In their way of thinking, compromise is a sign of weakness. Hitler, Stalin, and Mao began their political careers as terrorists. This fact is a further reason why diplomacy—I mean here, true diplomacy, not the virtue-signalling of an unelected elitist group who is only talking to the few like-minded, reinforcing their selfish sense of greatness and strength—is so important: to avoid a military conflict to break out in the first place. Only people who have survived a war know what ceasefire and peace mean.

Principle 5: "No state shall forcibly interfere in the constitution and government of another state." I think that this principle is very valid in an ideal world, but not in the real world, because it does not take into account the importance of political influence and the formation of alliances. In *Fauda*, the goals of Sunnite Hamas and Shiite Hezbollah are the same: financed by Iran, both terrorist groups pursue the extinction of Israel. What is the extinction of Israel? It is the total and complete forcible interference in Israel's constitution and government.

After the end of WWII, the Soviet Union militarily interfered in East Berlin in 1953, Budapest in 1956 and Prague in 1968. The Cold War can thus be identified as a long ceasefire, not peace. If I keep forcibly interfering in another state's government and constitution, no peace is realistic; my actions provoke the forcible reaction of my enemy or, at least, the hatred and contempt of the citizens of the state I interfere with. Ceasefire is not peace, but, more often than not, the most realistic solution.

Principle 6: "No state at war with another shall permit such acts of hostility as would make mutual confidence impossible during a future time of peace. Such acts would include the employment of assassins (*percussores*) or poisoners (*venefici*), breach of agreements, the instigation of treason (*perduellio*) within the enemy state, etc."

This principle is, like principles 1 and 5, outdated because to keep the ceasefire, I have to know what my enemy is up to. In *Fauda*, Israel's point of view is the following: I can protect my constitution, my citizens, and our state only with information. I must have as much information as possible to anticipate my enemy's plans, and this requires information-gathering, espionage, and the elimination of ideological leaders of terrorist groups. From Hamas and Hezbollah's point of view, the same applies for the continuation of their existence and the pursuit of their principal goal—to throw the Jews into the Mediterranean Sea. Therefore, I argue that Kant's principle 6 is outdated, because it ignores what is required to keep the ceasefire: information. To renounce on information is vital for me as a state.

To win the peace is quite another issue. One way of winning the peace, or rather, the ceasefire, was the Marshall plan of 1948: the material reconstruction of war-torn Europe was a generous activity that created trust among the Europeans, exhausted by WWII. They experienced the Western way of life, market economy and democracy and accepted it as viable alternative.

In the absence of hope for peace, there is but one way: political realism. One must be watchful, stay alert, be prepared for the worst, while hoping for the best. This means to educate each new generation about the dangers that are looming, without pushing them into becoming radicals, following an ideology. Such a fine line is best taught by history teachers. A history teacher who deserves this name educates young people to become responsible and democratic citizens, not uncritical subjects, or fanatical terrorists.

Fauda is a superbly written series, which portrays the difficulties of the Shin Bet team members in their operations and private lives. I especially liked the humanistic portrayal of the enemy: Abu Ahmad, Walid, Nidal al-Makdasi, Abu Samara, Abu Maher, Omar and Adel are portrayed as human beings with their own agendas, wishes and hopes. So are the team members, principal among them the hothead Doron and Gabi, the most dangerous operator at HQ.

Why is Gabi dangerous? Because he knows the Palestinian terrorists' mindset like the back of his hand, and he is ruthless. The team's enemies are certainly radicals, but they are portrayed with respect. The screen writers, among them Lior Raz who plays Doron, never ridicule the Palestinians, avoiding a cheap and superficial black and white view—on the contrary: they portray them as human beings who adhere to a different moral codex. All characters are convincing in their own specific ways of dealing with stress, violence, brutality, terror, and pain. The characters are created with depth and psychological acumen, and this allows the viewer to understand the arguments of Israel's enemies and the Israeli view of the conflict.

The series has taught me a lot about the human side of the conflict and enabled me to make a judgement for myself. According to Hannah Arendt, the will or reason not to cast judgement, *Urteilsenthaltung,* originates in one's individual capacity of thinking:

> "How troubled men of our time are by this question of judgement (or, as it is often said, by people who dare 'sit in judgement') has emerged in the controversy over the present book [...] The argument that we cannot judge if we were not present and involved ourselves seems to convince everyone everywhere, although it seems obvious that if it were true, neither the administration

of justice nor the writing of history would ever be possible." [58]

If I am right that family is the principal factor in this conflict that has been lasting since 1948, the best we can hope for is a stable ceasefire and the economic reconstruction of Lebanon, the neighbour in the North, and the Palestinian territories of the West Bank and Gaza. It is a sad fact that peace is no alternative for the Middle East. Too much blood has been shed on both sides, but Israel is a sovereign state. As the only democracy in the region, Israel has the right to defend herself.[59]

---

[58] Hannah Arendt, *Eichmann in Jerusalem* (Penguin: New York, 2006), 295-296.

[59] Israel is at war since 7 October 2023. It has been attacking Gaza, which has prompted mass protests in Western capitals such as London, Washington D.C., Sidney, and Berlin. I finished this text on 14 January 2024. Israel is being massively criticized for the bombing of Gaza, while Western pro Hamas activists are engaging in the support of "pre-civilizational massacre" (Victor Davis Hanson) that happened on 7 October. The slogan "From the river to the sea, Palestine will be free" is being chanted at gatherings, and antisemitism is rising. The slogan 'Never again', referring to the Holocaust, is now being replaced by 'Never again is now.'

IV. Antique Concepts of Love and Hatred: *The Lost Daughter*

> "Pregnancy and motherhood are experienced in very different ways depending on whether they take place in revolt, resignation, satisfaction, or enthusiasm. [...] Ordinarily, maternity is a strange compromise of narcissism, altruism, dream, sincerity, bad faith, devotion and cynicism".[1]

Introduction

Leda: "I am a non-natural mother."[2] In this interdisciplinary essay, combining plot analysis with philosophical analysis, I address this year's CONEXUS theme LOVE AND HATE with an inquiry into Maggie Gyllenhaal's film *The Lost Daughter* (2021), further referred to as TLD.[3] The film's plot is based on the novel of the same name by Italian author Elena Ferrante,[4] a pseudonym.

In part I, I elaborate on Hannah Arendt's (1906–1975) analysis of Augustine's concept of love and Plutarch's definition of hate, rendering the concepts operational for the

---

[1] Simone de Beauvoir, "The Mother", in *The Second Sex* (New York: Vintage, 2011), 535-584, 546, 570.
[2] The Lost Daughter, 11:46. Netflix's counting system is backwards; the time stamp indicates that there are 11 minutes and 46 seconds to watch until the end of the film.
[3] Information about the plot and the actors can be found on https://www.imdb.com/title/tt9100054/; accessed 13 October 2022.
[4] For a biography of the author see https://en.wikipedia.org/wiki/Elena_Ferrante; accessed 13 October 2022.

analysis of the plot. The definition of guilt is from Merriam-Webster online. Part II comprises a detailed presentation of the plot. In part III, I apply the definitions of love, hate and guilt to single scenes, trying to explain the emotions of the *personae* of TLD. I thus check the plot's presentations of love, hate, and guilt according to the definitions given in part I. Can we find both thinkers' definitions illustrated by the plot?

In the conclusion, I proceed to connect my plot analysis with the human extinction movement VHMET, [5] inquiring if the plot has theoretical elements in common with the movement. Lastly, I shall attempt to answer my two research questions: First, scrutinizing the human extinction movement, also referred to as anti-natalism: is the idea that mankind should render itself extinct a philosophical question? Second, is an individual's deliberate, hence rational, refusal to create offspring legitimate in ethical and political terms?

I Definitions

Hannah Arendt's definition of love[6] and Plutarch's (46–119) definition of hate[7] serve as the philosophical backbones of my analysis. I have chosen these two thinkers because Plutarch is a philosopher and Arendt a political theoretician;[8]

---

[5] The website of the movement is https://www.vhemt.org
[6] Arendt, *Love and Saint Augustine* (Chicago: University of Chicago Press, 1998).
[7] Plutarch, *Moralia, vol. VII*, (Harvard: Harvard University Press, 1959).
[8] Arendt said in the famous interview with Günther Gaus that she sees herself as a political theoretician, since the concept of 'political philosophy' was invalidated by Plato. Since Plato, thinking about politics cannot be neutral because political thinkers and theorists are

as I am no trained psychologist, I approach the emotions of love and hate from a philosophical point of view. Note that I use the modern Merriam-Webster description *qua* definition of the concept of 'guilt'.

Love

What is love? Arendt once said that one cannot love countries, states, or food, that is, things, objects. According to her, one can only love human beings:

> I have never in my life 'loved' some nation or collective— not the German, French or American nation, or the working class, or whatever else there might be in this price range of loyalties. The fact is that I love only my friends.[9]

Arendt thus distinguishes between love and loyalty: I love my friends, but I am loyal to my fatherland, joining, for example, the military. I love my parents, but my loyalty to my university makes me join my alma mater's annual volleyball

---

principally interested in the normative good, the ethical side of politics, thus the search for a morally good political system. The interview was broadcast on NDR (Norddeutscher Rundfunk) in 1964, https://www.youtube.com/watch?v=J9SyTEUi6Kw; accessed 19 November 2022.

[9] Marie-Louise Knott, ed., *The Correspondence of Hannah Arendt and Gershom Scholem* (Chicago: The University of Chicago Press, 20179, 206. Arendt's definition thus refers to the feeling of love as exclusively defined between human beings. If I have understood her correctly, a human being can also love an animal, because the animal, my dog or cat, is an animated being, it has a soul and is alive, not an object like a dish or a vase. I thank the anonymous reviewer for his/her suggestion.

competition. I eat Japanese sushi daily, but that is not love; it is a personal culinary preference. I love my siblings, while I have feelings of sympathy or friendship for my colleagues at work.

Furthermore, I deem it safe to ascertain that we in the English-speaking world use the concept of love not only in an inflationary way, but often also incorrectly. Indeed, the L word seems to be everywhere today; even the slogan of a US fast food chain uses 'love' to advertise its burgers, milkshakes, and fries. By contrast, the ancient Greeks had six concepts for love: *eros, philia, ludus, agape, pragma,* and *philautia.*[10]

Let us now look at Arendt's definition of love, based on her philosophical analysis of Augustine. Note that I fully rely on Arendt, as I am no specialist in Greek antique philosophy or early Christian thought. According to Arendt, Augustine

---

[10] *Eros* is sexual passion; *philia* is deep friendship; *ludus* is playful love, as, for example, the playful affection of children or adults engaging in flirting; *agape* is selfless love or empathy, the love for everyone; *pragma* is the mature, realistic love of an old married couple that knows how to compromise to keep the relationship stable, and *philautia* is self-love. The six forms of Greek love on https://www.yesmagazine.org/health-happiness/2013/12/28/the-ancient-greeks-6-words-for-love-and-why-knowing-them-can-change-your-life; accessed 23 November 2022. My esteemed colleague Sebastian Florian Weiner, adjunct professor of antique philosophy at UZH, comments on the source's interpretation of *philautia*: "The Aristotelian self-love is not quite correctly presented here. Aristotle thinks that *philautia* begins once man acts morally, because one aims at one's own good as one's personal goal or achievement. Aristotle does not distinguish *philautia* from narcissism, as the author claims. Therefore, one can state that in Aristotle's thinking the virtuous person can become narcissistic, seeking in the other his 'own self'."—email conversation with Weiner from 19 to 23 November 2022.

defines love as appearing[11] in two forms: love can appear either in the form of *caritas* or as *cupiditas*.[12] A summary of the complicated relationship of man with God, other men, and the world:

> "The world is constituted as an earthly world not just by the works of God but by the 'lovers of the world', that is, by men, and by what they love. [...] The right love consists in the right object. Mortal man, who has been placed into the world (here understood as heaven and earth) and must leave it, instead clings to it and in the process turns the world itself into a vanishing one, that is, one due to vanish with his death. The specific identification of earthly and mortal is possible only if the world is seen from the point of view of mortal man. Augustine's term for this wrong, mundane love that clings to, and thus at the same time constitutes, the world is cupiditas. In contrast, the right love seeks

---

[11] What renders Arendt's analysis of Augustine so complicated is the blend of three currents of philosophy: first, Arendt's analysis of Augustine's antique Greek philosophy, second, her analysis of Augustine's early Christian thinking, and third, Arendt's own approach from a philosophical point of view that is close to phenomenological thought. I think Martin Heidegger (1889–1976), Arendt's doctor father, inspired her with his subjective phenomenology, which was developed from Edmund Husserl's (1859–1938) initial phenomenology. Thus, we have three different philosophical systems blended into one analysis: Antique Greek philosophy, early Christian philosophy, and modern phenomenological thought. For a brief overview of the distinction between Heidegger' subjective phenomenology and Jan Patočka's (1907–1977) asubjective phenomenology, see my *Politik als praktizierte Sittlichkeit. Zum Demokratiebegriff bei Thomas G. Masaryk und Václav Havel* (Sinzheim: Pro Universitate Verlag, 1998), 254-259.

[12] Arendt, *Saint Augustine*, 17.

eternity and the absolute future. Augustine calls this right love caritas: the 'root of all evil is cupiditas, the root of all good is caritas'. However, both right and wrong love (caritas and cupiditas) have this in common—craving desire, that is appetitus. Hence, Augustine warns, 'Love, but be careful what you love.'"[13]

Now, how to explain a parent's love for his child with Augustine? If I am allowed a simple definition of parental love as evidence of mankind's biological drive to procreation, hence a natural instinct, I can say: parental love is in Augustine's sense the right love that seeks eternity and the absolute future. What do eternity and absolute future mean in the context of human procreation? They are, at the same time, the goal and instrument of the survival of the species *homo sapiens*. If I have children, I secure the survival of the species, and my offspring will do the same, thus steer the species towards eternity and the absolute future, i.e., the abstract and unknown future. Our understanding of the past, that is history, and the future, that is an unknown place, is being made by us now, in the present. Therefore, we know the past, but cannot explain or predict the future. We do not know what is going to happen in the years ahead; all we can do is make an educated guess that originates in our memory of the past, hence our empirical memory, what we have experienced. I assume that my children will procreate as I did, and before me, my parents, and grandparents. To sum up,

---

[13] Arendt, *Saint Augustine*, 17. Her first reference: *Commentaries* on the Psalms, 90, I, 8; the second reference: *Commentaries*, 34, 5c.

we could say that *caritas* is geared towards God; it is a kind of metaphysical instrument and goal at the same time.

What is *cupiditas*? According to Augustine, it is the wrong love and thus source of all evil, yet it is, like *caritas*, the constituent of the world, the evil pillar of the world. Notice the duality of Christian thinking. *Cupiditas* is bad, and it does exist as a counterpart to the good, to *caritas*. If parental love is the constituent of the good, that is, the connection of man with God, *cupiditas* is, if I am correct, the bad love that makes man covet earthly things, a bad desire, because it is shallow, finite and, at the end of the day, superficial. What are superficial objects of bad love, bad coveting? I think such objects of desire can be defined as not related to God, thus related to man's desire only, a selfish desire for objects here and now on earth. For example, if I covet an earthly object, I do not connect with God, but to something that keeps me from connecting with God: it distracts me from the good path, the good love towards God. Whether I desire a Bugatti motorcycle, or a pair of Gucci shoes does not play a role at all—they are the objects of my selfish desire. If I engage in an extra-marital affair, such a relationship does not connect with God; it originates in my selfish desire for this person. My desire, my *appetitus*, my coveting of material objects or human objects hinders me from connecting with God; therefore, my desire for such objects is a sign of my selfishness.

Now, how would Arendt with Augustine explain marriage? She did not mention the love between husband and wife in her analysis, but I think that she would say that Augustine would conceive of marriage, because it is blessed by God, also as *caritas*, the condition necessary for having children, thus an activity that shall render possible *caritas* as parental love. Augustine did not define friendship, sympathy, being in love or the end of marriage. Quite naturally, according to the thinking of his times, Augustine did not elaborate on the end of marriage as connection with God, because in his times, it simply did not exist. Couples, once married, lived together, brought up their offspring, and then died. Unlike in Judaism, which acknowledged divorce in biblical times, Christianity recognized divorce as legal and legitimate only after the French Revolution of 1789.

What is divorce? It is the earthly, legal end of the marriage contract and, also, an act and decision that renders the Church's blessing of the marriage null and void. I think that Augustine, catapulted into our 21st century, would not understand why a couple files for divorce. Why, their bond is made in heaven, blessed by God via the Church, so how can they go against what God protects and blesses? I think Augustine would not have understood that marriage can end with both ex-spouses still alive and more often happier than before.

Hate

Plutarch distinguishes between envy and hate, which he considered as two bad passions, indeed, vices as the opposite of virtues:

> "The intention of the hater is to injure, and the meaning of hate is thus defined: it is a certain disposition and intention, awaiting the opportunity to injure. In envy

this, at any rate, is absent. For there are many of their intimates and connexions that the envious would not be willing to see destroyed or suffer misfortune, although tormented by their good fortune; and while they abridge their fame and glory if they can, they would not, on the other hand, afflict them with irreparable calamities, but as with a house towering above their own, are content to pull down the part that casts them in the shade."[14]

According to Plutarch, hate is a strong passion or emotion that makes me want to destroy the object of my hate, to afflict irreparable damage to another person. One can hate other human beings and also irrational animals, hence creatures that lack reason, *logos,* the human capacity for thinking.[15] If I hate my neighbour, I am thus consciously and deliberately ready, intent on killing this person or inflicting irreparable damage to his body and mind. If I am envious, the intention to destroy is absent. I envy my neighbour's large mansion because I want to have a mansion like him. When I envy my teacher's intellect and wisdom, I want to be as wise and intelligent as she is. When I hate, I am intent on destroying; when I envy, I covet, I desire what the other has. From this follows that envy occurs only between man and man.

Plutarch's wise words furthermore state that one can say openly that one hates, but with regard to envy, things are more complicated: nobody wants to admit that he or she is

---

[14] Plutarch, *Moralia VII*, 107.
[15] Plutarch, *Moralia VII*, 97: "Some people hate weasels, beetles, toads, or snakes."

envious, since to do so would make one look bad, petty and weak:

> "[...] is the circumstance that while some confess that they hate a good many people, there is no one that they will say they envy [...] cloaking and concealing their envy with whatever other name occurs to them for their passion, implying that among the disorders of the soul it is alone unmentionable."[16]

Envy is therefore a feeling that begets, requires, needs secrecy. It is a hidden feeling and thought, hidden in my brain and heart. I conceal my envy because to say to my neighbour that I am envious of her large mansion would prompt her to think of me as a petty and weak person, a loser who is incapable of making the money to buy such a mansion—and the neighbour would be spot on. It would also arouse pity for me, and nobody wants to be pitied, because pity can also be a mild form of contempt.

Guilt

My last definition is 'guilt': The Merriam-Webster online dictionary defines 'guilt' in three forms:

> First, the fact of having committed a breach of conduct especially violating law and involving a penalty. Second a, the state of one who has committed an offense especially consciously. Second b, feelings of deserving blame especially for imagined offenses or from a sense

---

[16] Plutarch, *Moralia VII*, 97.

of inadequacy, self-reproach. Third, a feeling of deserving blame for offenses.[17]

'Guilt' is defined first in legal terms, second a, as a psychological state of mind, second b, as feelings of personal inferiority, of not being good enough, or as feeling of regret of my inferiority, that is self-reproach. Third and lastly, guilt is defined as a feeling of understanding that I have done wrong. Let me explain this modern definition of guilt.

First, a court declares me guilty, because it has proof that I, for example, killed my neighbour's cat. The proof can be an eyewitness or the shotgun that has my fingerprints on it. Second a, I feel guilty after having stolen my colleague's bike. I know that stealing is an offense, but I did it anyway to get to the railway station in time. Second b, guilt as self-reproach: I could have decided not to lie to my parents, but I did lie to them, and therefore, I reproach myself *ex post* for lying to Mom and Dad. And third, lastly, if I am feeling guilty, I am consciously aware that I have done wrong. This consciousness of having committed a crime or violated society's normative, moral rules, makes me accept the punishment. Why? I accept the punishment, because I understand that I did wrong and, therefore, have to be punished. Let us now look at the plot of *The Lost Daughter*.

II *The Lost Daughter*—the Plot

In the early hours of the morning, at dawn, we see a woman with short black hair getting out of her car. She is walking

---

[17] The noun 'guilt' on https://www.merriam-webster.com/dictionary/guilt; accessed 16 November 2023.

towards the beach and is visibly unstable on her feet. Probably in her late forties, she wears a white linen shirt and skirt. She stumbles onto the beach and collapses into the surf.

As we later learn, Leda, portrayed by Olivia Colman, is a 48-year-old professor of translation and specialist in Italian poetry and literature. She arrives on a Greek island in the summer. She meets the house carer Lyle, played by Ed Harris; Lyle helps her with the luggage. The viewer's first impression: Leda is an attractive, self-confident, and intelligent woman, but prefers to keep to herself. She is not interested in making friends, but she obeys the common rules of social manners.

The next morning, Leda goes to the beach, carrying a large beach tote with books and notebooks. She is preparing a course she is going to teach in the autumn term. Will, the young man who works at the beach hut sells her ice cream, and they have a friendly chat.

With a lot of pomp, a loud and imposing clan from New Jersey arrives on the beach. Leda is annoyed by their noise, trying to focus on her work. She spots a beautiful young mother with a five-year-old daughter; they are members of the clan. The way the little girl clings to her mother, constantly demanding her attention, reminds Leda of something. She has tears in her eyes. The viewer does not know yet why Leda is sad, but one understands that the young mother and the girl remind her of something painful in her past.

The next day, Leda is again on the beach, and a huge boat arrives, spilling out even noisier people, carrying sound machines. They are the clan's birthday guests. Callie, played by Dagmara Dominczyk, the highly pregnant wife of the clan's boss, is organizing her 40th birthday. They are preparing a beach party, asking the tourists on the beach to make room for the party guests. Everybody obliges to Callie's wish, moving their umbrellas and beach stuff away, but Leda is the only one who refuses. When Callie with her protruding belly—it is quite vulgar, almost obscene[18] how Callie demonstrates her pregnancy showing off her naked belly for all to see—approaches Leda, asking her in a kind but determined tone if she could move, Leda politely refuses. No thanks, she is fine where she is. This public show of self-confidence and open resistance against being bullied leaves Callie rather surprised and frustrated, and she admits that she does not know what to say to Leda. Clearly, Callie is a woman who is used to getting what she wants. She is complaining angrily to the clan's men, old and young, using foul language, until her husband Vassili, the clan's boss, tells her to stop.

After an hour, Callie approaches Leda, carrying a saucer with a piece of birthday cake; she apologizes, and they begin a conversation. Leda tells her that she was born in Leeds, UK, but lives in Cambridge, close to Boston. It is unclear if she teaches at Harvard University or another Bostonian college. Callie says she thought that Leda, because of her assertiveness, would be from Queens, New York. They speak

---

[18] A description and explanation of the adjective 'vulgar' on https://www.collinsdictionary.com/dictionary/english/vulgar; 'obscene' on https://www.collinsdictionary.com/dictionary/english/vulgar; both links accessed 26 November 2022. I have chosen these two adjectives because they best describe the sexualisation of Callie's pregnancy.

about children, and Leda expresses what we are going to understand as her personal tragedy in a short sentence: "Children are an excruciating responsibility."[19] If we take Leda's words seriously, and she is not, as we shall soon learn, one to make nonsensical small talk, she thus thinks that having children is close to torture, hence excruciating, the suffering of severe pain. What kind of torture? I think she means psychological torture.

Callie explains that her younger sister Nina, portrayed by Dakota Johnson, became pregnant immediately while she had to be patient for many years. Nina is the young mother with the clingy daughter Leda has observed the first morning. Callie asks Leda, if she has children, and Leda replies that her elder daughter Bianca is 25 years old and Marta two years younger. The two ladies part in an amicable fashion.

While she is walking back to her flat, a pinecone hits Leda, and she has a large wound on her back. She does not care and goes down to the bar for dinner. Caretaker Lyle is sitting there with his friends, playing cards, and drinking ouzo. He approaches her in his usual friendly manner, and it is obvious that he is interested in her. Leda replies with short sentences and then dismisses him; she wants to finish her dinner. Lyle is hurt and goes back to his friends.

What happens then is still quite a mystery to me in psychological terms from the point of view of the *persona* Leda: as if she had a bad conscience about having been so unfriendly to Lyle, Leda goes over to the men, stands behind Lyle, spies into his cards and then whispers into his ear

---

[19] 1:41:06.

"bellissimo gioco",[20] which means "a most beautiful game" in Italian. Then she apologizes, grabs her handbag and storms out of the bar. Why does she act like this? Is she semi-autistic? Why does she violate Lyle's personal boundaries by whispering in Italian to him and then apologizes? Or is Leda bi-polar, suffering from mood swings? It is not likely that Lyle, an American who speaks Greek because he has been living on the island for more than thirty years understands Italian. She speaks to him in the language in which she has made her academic career, her professional life. Is she showing off, presenting her academic acumen? Her rushing out looks to us as if she is fleeing from her herself, from her recent intrusion into Lyle's personal space, her violation of his personal boundaries.

The next morning, Leda observes Nina and her handsome husband fighting on the beach. Then, the clan is in turmoil: little daughter Elena is missing. Leda has a flashback: she remembers that years ago, her elder daughter Bianca went missing on a beach, and she, carrying little Marta in her arms, was frantically looking for Bianca. She helps the clan in its search. Nina is shouting Elena's name hysterically. Leda, guided by her instincts, goes to a part of the beach that is hidden by a little forest. There, she finds Elena and brings her back to Nina. Little Elena is crying incessantly because she cannot find her doll. Leda is now the clan's hero, and Callie, spotting the wound on Leda's back, applies some cream, instructing her how long to use it.

---

[20] 1:37:58.

Upon learning that Elena is missing her doll, Leda has another flashback: she remembers that she had given her beloved doll Mena to little Bianca, who had painted the doll with some colours—Mena was ruined, and young mother Leda, in a spur of anger, hate, and hurt, had shouted at Bianca and then thrown Mena out of the window. Her beloved doll broke into pieces on the street, gone forever. This act seems to me like young mother Leda had said a painful good-bye to her childhood after Bianca had ruined her doll.

Later, Leda finds Elena's doll on the beach and quickly shovels her into her handbag. We do not yet understand why she doesn't return the doll immediately to the clan, knowing that everybody is looking for it.

In the evening, Leda goes on a sightseeing tour through the village and meets young Will, the beach caretaker, at the port. She invites him to dinner, and they have a nice conversation, much as if Will was the boyfriend of Bianca or Marta, Leda thus a kind of mother-in-law to him. She is opening up to Will and tells him about Bianca and Marta. Then, she asks him about the clan. Will tells her that the clan lives in the pink villa above the village. Complimenting her on her courage in having stood up to Callie's bullying yesterday on the beach, he warns her not to do this again because "they are bad people".[21]

The next day, Leda visits a children's toy shop. Her intention, as we understand, is to buy new clothes for the doll that is dirty and dishevelled. Upon paying, she runs into

---

[21] 1:18:44.

Callie, her husband and Nina, who is carrying Elena. The clan wants to buy Elena a new doll, to make her stop crying. It is visible how unnerved Nina is by her daughter—the young mother is at the end of her tether. She has a nervous, exhausted, and guilty look on her face which prompts a flashback in Leda: she remembers that one day Bianca so got on her nerves that she shouted at her little girl. Indeed, director Gyllenhaal captured that moment perfectly: the viewer can sympathize with young Leda. The constant whiny crying of little Bianca got on my nerves too. One just wants to shout 'Leave me alone! Stop crying! Be quiet!' Imagine having to endure a little child's crying while you are working on an academic paper!

By now, we know that young Leda was pursuing a career in academia, trying to concentrate on her work with two little daughters distracting her all the time. They used to play a game: the girls asked her to do the snake, upon which Leda used to peel an orange without breaking the peel into little pieces, which made the peel look like a snake. Young Leda, portrayed by Jessie Buckley, conceived of Bianca as a problematic child, while the younger Marta was practically non-existent. Shy, quiet, and reclusive Marta is an obedient and self-effacing child, respecting her mother's needs for her personal and professional space. Marta is the opposite of loud, pushy, and provocative Bianca.

Walking home to her flat, Leda remembers another episode in her life: she and husband Joe, who is also a young academic, pursuing his career, are on holiday with their daughters in a hut, when Joe, portrayed by Jack Farthing, spots some hikers who are lost. They invite the couple in and after the daughters have been put to bed the four have dinner together. The young woman tells Leda and Joe about their love story: when she met her man, he was married with three children, but fate had brought them together. He left his wife and children and has been with her ever since. Leda and the female hiker like each other instantly, because the female hiker is Italian, complimenting young Leda on her superb knowledge of Italian literature and poetry. The next morning, the hiking couple leaves, and the Italian asks Leda for copies of her work. Young Leda is happy at being acknowledged as a serious academic.

When Leda gets back home to her holiday flat, she takes the doll out of the cupboard where she has hidden it and puts it on the table on her balcony, planning to wash it and put on the new clothes she has just bought. The doorbell rings. It is Lyle, offering Leda freshly caught octopus; Lyle invites himself to cook dinner for them. They drink wine and ouzo with the meal. They talk about meanness and cruelty, accusing themselves of being mean and cruel—that is the one thing they have in common. Why? We learn from their conversation that Lyle has left his wife and three children in Philadelphia to be on his own on the island. Leda is a bit dizzy from the ouzo and lies her head on Lyle's shoulder, which is again a violation of his personal boundaries. He does not mind. She falls asleep; when she wakes up, she sees Lyle smoking on the balcony and knows that he has seen the doll on the table. As the caretaker, Lyle knows the clan and is, like everybody in the village, aware that they are looking for the doll. He does not comment nor ask Leda why she has the doll; he simply says that the doll is full of water.

The next day, Leda walks up to the pink villa where the clan resides. She has seen many flyers attached to trees in the little forest above the beach and decides in the spur of the moment to call Nina, most probably to tell her that she has found Elena's doll. One senses that Leda is attracted by Nina in a motherly way. Does Nina remind her of Bianca? Leda hears voices and then, through some trees, sees Nina kissing Will, the young caretaker of the beach.

This sexual scene prompts a flashback in Leda: the young mother is working on a text with her headphones on, while the daughters are playing in a room close to her study. As husband Joe has accepted a position at a Canadian university, she is alone with the children, carrying the burden of a single mother. She cannot concentrate on her text and begins to masturbate, when the daughters rush in and interrupt her—the phone is ringing. Leda rushes to pick up the phone and is delighted to learn that she is invited to a conference, hotel and travel expenses paid by the organizers. She instructs the nanny about the daughter's eating habits and leaves.

At the conference, Professor Hardy, played by Peter Sarsgaard praises her recently published paper, and she joins him and his friends for dinner. Professor Hardy and young Leda get on like a house on fire and end up kissing on the staircase when everybody has gone to bed. We see a young and happy Leda, acknowledged as an academic and courted by an older academic who appreciates her research.

In the evening, Leda decides to go to the local cinema. A group of teenage boys are rushing in, making a lot of noise. So unnerved and angry is Leda about this foul behaviour that she shouts at them—to no avail. The boys keep disturbing the public's view of the film. Leda leaves the theatre and talks to the usher, asking her to fix the problem. The boys start to behave only once Vassili, the clan's boss and Callie's husband, intervenes and tells them to shut up. Here, I had the impression that the boss is keeping a watchful eye on Leda. What are his motives? Is he grateful to Leda because she found Elena, expressing his gratitude by protecting her? Or is he suspicious of her, following her around? Vassili's intervention at the cinema makes Leda remember her past: she has begun a love affair with Professor Hardy and stays with him, making husband Joe come back to Boston to take care of their daughters.

The next day, Leda visits the local market at the port. Her phone rings. It is Nina, who wants to talk to her. Leda tells her where she is, and after a couple of minutes, Nina joins her at a stall with antique trinkets. Nina tells her that she knows that Leda has seen her with Will, acknowledging her affair. Nina is wearing a large straw hat, a gift from her husband, who is away during the week, probably doing some shady business. The wind keeps blowing the hat away, and Leda, much like a caring mother, buys a hatpin and fixes Nina's hat. Clearly, Nina admires the older woman for her self-confidence and asks her what had happened to her in the doll shop. Nina is a sensitive young woman; in the toy shop, she felt that there was something going on in Leda. Leda replies, explaining her memory with tears in her eyes: "I abandoned them and didn't see them for three years. I left."[22] She admits that the three years with Professor Hardy were wonderful,

---

[22] 30:17.

amazing, she felt she was able to be herself again. The girls were seven and five years old, when she left them.

In the evening, Leda explores the village. She spots Lyle, dancing on his own in a local square. The whole village is there, participating in a social event: grandmothers and grandfathers, babies, children, teenagers, and middle-aged couples. This local event is, I think, a symbol for the family as the unity of everything, of human life and social order. Everybody loves the music and the dancing. Leda is wearing a red dress and looks very beautiful. Lyle asks her to join in the dancing; she is having a great time, dancing, and flirting with him. Suddenly, as if some Greek gods had cast a dark shadow on the happy village community, Lyle tells Leda to leave now: the clan has arrived. It is as if the clan is the epitome of evil: everybody is afraid of them, feeling uncomfortable when they show up.

Leda, taking Lyle's warning seriously, walks back home. Young Will is standing in front of her door, asking her if she could leave her flat to him and Nina for some hours of privacy. Leda replies that she would like to talk to Nina about this.

In the morning, Nina visits Leda in her flat. She tells her that she has not much time, having given Callie an excuse and leaving little Elena with her. When Nina asks Leda if this will ever stop, referring to her daughter's exhausting need for constant attention, her own exhaustion and guilt about her exhaustion, Leda replies in a non-committal way. In this scene, I had the impression that Leda was not interested in the feelings of the young mother. Leda seems to be hot and cold; on the one hand, she takes care of Nina, buying her the hatpin. On the other hand, she seems remote and does not really engage with the young mother's sadness. Then, Nina asks her why she went back to her daughters. With tears in her eyes, Leda replies: "I am their mother. I went back because I missed them. I am a very selfish person."[23] Much as if she had realized her bad behaviour, her cruel and mean hiding of the doll, Leda gets up and gives Elena's doll to Nina, telling her: "I am a non-natural mother".[24] Nina is so shocked about Leda having hidden the doll that, on the spur of a moment, she storms out, then returns, shouting at Leda that she wants nothing from her, pulling out the hatpin from her hat and pushing it into Leda's stomach. She leaves the keys to the flat on the table and storms out for good.

In the last scene, at night, we see Leda pushing her two large suitcases down the stairs, getting into her rental car and driving away. She is driving semi-consciously, erratically. She stops at the beach, gets out of the car, stumbles on to the beach and collapses into the surf. In the morning, a huge wave splashes into Leda's face, waking her up. Is she dead? Is what we see her immortal soul if we believe in the immortality of the soul? Leda calls Bianca: Hi, it's Mum. We hear Bianca replying that she thought Leda was dead. All of a sudden, Leda has an orange in her hand, smiles happily, keeps talking to Bianca on the phone and begins to peel the orange like she did when the daughters were little, making a snake of the peel. Again, in this final scene, it is Bianca that gets all of Leda's attention. Where is Marta?

---

[23] 13:05
[24] 11:46.

The plot's denouement that makes sense to me, since it explains the film's main tenet and the novel's title: the lost daughter is Marta, the forgotten child. Leda does not even have a bad conscience, a feeling of guilt of forgetting Marta, so focussed on, almost mesmerized is she with rebellious Bianca. Bianca is the centre and epitome of Leda's *caritas*, hate, self-anger and self-reproach, the subject of her guilty conscience as a mother. Marta is lost to Leda because of Leda's fixation on Bianca, and the most painful character trait of Leda's we can observe is that she is not even aware that she has lost her second child due to her overbearing *caritas* for her first. If I am not aware that I have lost somebody, I have no regrets, no feelings of guilt. I am blissfully ignorant of that which other persons, more self-aware and less selfish than me, would regret as a loss.

III Arendt and Augustine's Love, Plutarch's Hate, and Guilt as Self-Reproach

I have selected several situations of the plot and proceed now to the analysis of these situations.

Love

Quite obviously, Leda expresses her love for Bianca whenever she speaks about her, praising her strong character. This is Leda's *caritas*. As I have mentioned before, Marta does not get the attention Leda pays to Bianca. Leda mentions shy Marta too, but not with the emotions she has for Bianca, much as if Marta was just there, a little extension of Bianca, a little thing worthy of mention by name only.

There is no detailed description of her character, just the factual, rational acknowledgement that little Marta exists, that she has two daughters.

Another scene demonstrating love as *cupiditas* is Leda's affair with the professor. She has left her family to be with him. The Greeks would call this feeling *eros*, sexual passion. They do not marry but live together for three years. She does not have children with the professor; according to Augustine, he was thus a source of evil love, meaning, the object of her selfishness, her selfish craving for happiness, sexual fulfilment, independence, and professional acknowledgement. The professor provides her with what she desires in professional terms: contacts, acknowledgement, and time for her research. Her love for him is *cupiditas*; the professor is the object of her selfish desire. We do not know whether the professor is married and leaves his wife for Leda; if this is the case, young Leda is the object of his *cupiditas*.

The hiking couple who has dinner with young Leda and husband Mike in the holiday cabin portray the love between a man and a woman that destroys families, since the man has left his family for her. This is *cupiditas*. Had they married in church and had children together, their love would have turned from *cupiditas* to *caritas*, a new cycle of parental love that would have connected them with God. But they did not. The Italian woman's selfish love for a married man is what young Leda experiences with the professor: the selfish happiness that originates in carelessness, or the renouncing of one's responsibilities, the ignoring of one's duties to, according to Augustine, one's family and God. The Greeks would refer to this kind of love as *eros*, while Augustine with

Arendt calls it *cupiditas,* evil love. In the last scene, when she is dead, Leda calls Bianca on her mobile phone, peeling an orange. I think this scene is a symbol of her motherly love for Bianca, her *caritas* for her first child.

Nina's admiration for Leda, the older self-assured woman, could be referred to as a blend of *agape* and *philia*, a deep feeling of sympathy and empathy, non-sexual love. Augustine's definitions of *caritas* and *cupiditas* do not apply to this relationship. Nina is the only one who senses Leda's self-reproach, her guilt. This requires empathy, a general interest in another human being. Also, we could refer to the Italian's feelings for young Leda, whom she has just met at the holiday cabin and spent some hours with her, as *philia*. If I am correct, *philia* is more personal, that is, directed toward one's object of one's love, while *agape* is more general, extending to mankind, to many.

Hate

Naturally, Nina pushing the hatpin into Leda's stomach is an act of hate; she wants to destroy her, because Leda has hidden Elena's doll from the clan, although everybody knew they were frantically looking for it. First, upon seeing the doll in Leda's hands, Nina is confused and asks the elder woman why she hid the doll. Leda replies that she is a non-natural mother. This answer makes Nina so angry that she pushes the hatpin into Leda. Hate can flare up in microseconds. Why does Leda's answer make Nina so angry? Remember, she admired the older woman's courage and education, looking up to her as a motherly figure.

I interpret this scene as follows, and, naturally, my interpretation is speculation: it could very well be possible that Nina feels guilty because little Elena is getting on her nerves with her antics. Nina projects her self-reproach and self-anger on to Leda. Nina kills Leda because of her feeling of guilt: Leda's answer that she is a non-natural mother prompts anxiety and anger in Nina. Nina's guilt is caused by her almost visceral fear of not being good enough, of also being a non-natural mother, and this strong emotion transforms in microseconds into hatred of Leda. She thus kills the person who has reminded her of her guilt. Leda is the only one in the story who dies, and she dies at the hands of a clan member.

A further situation that demonstrates hate is, I think, the clan's behaviour toward the villagers. The clan members impose themselves on the villagers; they behave in a bossy and arrogant manner, ignoring other people's boundaries. Everybody on the beach has to move because of Callie's birthday party; when the villagers and tourists enjoy themselves dancing in the square, the happy atmosphere changes lightning fast with the arrival of the clan. I think that the clan's general perception of the world is based on mistrust, contempt, and the feeling 'us against the whole world', which we could interpret as a kind of proto-hate, a precursor of hatred of everybody who is not a member of the clan.

Guilt

Besides love and hate, guilt in the form of self-reproach is a very visible emotion in the plot. I think that guilt is the feeling that dominates the plot. Lyle senses that Leda and he have something in common, and he wants to find out what it is. He cooks dinner for them with freshly caught octopus. He confesses his guilt at having left his family in Philadelphia to be on his own on the island, but Leda does not divulge her own guilt to him. Both consider themselves cruel and mean persons—on this point they agree. That is the reason why Lyle does not ask Leda why Elena's doll is on her table on the balcony. He recognizes her selfishness and is not interested in her motives. Their personal fate is what they both understand and acknowledge in each other: selfishness, the origins of their cruel decisions and mean behaviour. They are mildly flirting while Lyle is cooking the octopus. The Greeks would call this activity of superficial playful flirting *ludus*.

I think what Leda and Lyle have in common is something deeper: human sympathy and empathy, which is *philia*, the non-sexual feeling of love and understanding of another human being. Both Lyle and Leda sense that they are equal in their guilt; they share the deep emotion of self-reproach. Lyle does not mention his guilt in words, *expressis verbis*, but his face—and this makes Harris such an accomplished, fine actor—displays his deep, devouring sense of guilt. Leda understands him because she has done the same to her family. Indeed, it must be psychological torture to feel guilty all the time for past decisions and choices, aware that one cannot leave one's skin, that one cannot forgive one's selfishness and move on.

We could further say that both Lyle and Leda are stuck in the past; their overwhelming feelings of guilt deny them happiness in the present and future. Perennial guilt as self-reproach must be a particular circle in Dante's hell.

A further scene that portrays guilt is Leda's attraction to Nina, the young mother. We could interpret their relationship as an *ersatz* mother-daughter relationship, which naturally ends with Nina killing Leda. Guilt is also the principal feeling that guides Leda; she feels this self-reproach all the time. She was selfish and left the family but came back after three years because she missed the daughters, she tells Nina. She confides her guilt to the young mother, answering her truthfully. Nina has touched something in Leda that makes her openly confess her innermost self to a person she has just met a couple of days ago. Nina is neither a friend nor a colleague, just a holiday acquaintance, but Leda trusts her, because she senses that Nina understands her guilt. Nina wants to understand herself and her own guilt about being unnerved with little Elena's antics; that is the reason why she seeks Leda's company.

Conclusion

May we live long and die out.[25]

This is the Voluntary Human Extinction Movement's (VHEMT) principal slogan. The movement explains its goal of mankind's self-extinction with the protection of the planet.

---

[25] The website of VHEMT on https://www.vhemt.org/logo.htm; accessed 24 November 2022. See also the NYT interview with Les Knight, the founder of the movement on https://www.nytimes.com/2022/11/23/climate/voluntary-human-extinction.html; accessed 25 November 2022.

Once the species *homo sapiens* is gone, once mankind has vanished from the earth driven by its own free will to die out, the blue planet shall be safe.

Thus, VHEMT does not advocate mass murder or mass suicide; to achieve its goal, the members simply declare that they renounce on having children, thus reject procreation. This is a personal choice that can turn into a political issue.

If I live in a democratic state and an open, tolerant society and decide not to have children, that is my personal choice. My government cannot make me produce children if I do not want to have any. Furthermore, in an open society, I can openly declare that having children is a crime towards the planet, making my personal belief a political statement. Who can prove the opposite and with what argument? In an open and tolerant society, any idea thus can be politicized. Another issue is how many individuals take my ideas seriously.

Now, the VHEMT's idea is certainly a universal one, because it reaches out to mankind. Yet, it is also utopian to the core, devoid of realistic consideration. How do people survive in poor Third World countries? Children are the only guarantee of the survival of the parents when they grow older. Poor states do not have social security systems and pension systems like the rich states of the West. Therefore, as a poor farmer in, for example, Bangladesh, I must have children to take care of me when I am old, ill, and frail. Procreation is thus the only means people in poor states have at their disposal; children and grandchildren are the instruments of the family's survival.

Are there elements of VHEMT to be found in TLD? Leda's guilt at having abandoned her children is certainly close to the question whether one should have children at all. Yet, the plot centres on Leda's guilt and her lack of awareness that she has lost her second child, not on the future of the planet and our species on it. Leda is torn between her *caritas* for Bianca and her guilt. We do not know if she has regrets at having produced two children, but she openly says to Callie that children are an excruciating responsibility, thus a responsibility that is torturous. It certainly takes a special character and mindset to leave one's young children for a love affair.

Furthermore, Leda self-identifies as being a non-natural mother—what does she mean? I think that she has the picture of the ideal mother in her mind, and that would be Mary, mother of God, the principal Christian symbol of femininity and icon of motherhood. Leda has been socialized in the Christian West. Saint Mary is the role model for all Christian women, leading by example through personal sacrifice, modesty, love for mankind and obedience to God. The perfect woman, the perfect mother, has only one child, the son of God, has conceived him without intercourse, and that is why Mary's heart and body are pure. This is an ideal Leda cannot reach, and she knows it. Her guilt is a daily torture. Therefore, the principal element of VHEMT, namely the deliberate decision not to have children to save the planet, cannot be found in the plot.

Let me now answer my research questions. First, scrutinizing the human extinction movement, also referred to as anti-natalism: is the idea that mankind should voluntarily render itself extinct a philosophical question?

Yes, absolutely. The central idea of the movement is a philosophical question, and a revolutionary one at that. I compare it with Jean-Jacques Rousseau's (1712–1778) critique of civilization, which, in his time, was revolutionary to the core and earned him, together with his enemy Voltaire (François-Marie Arouet, 1694–1778), a place in the pantheon in Paris. The post-revolutionary French nation expressed its reverence for these Enlightenment thinkers, placing them in adjacent tombs. Thus, Voltaire and Rousseau rest in perennial peace, facing each other.

Prior to Rousseau, the various themes philosophers and political thinkers since Plato and Aristotle were concerned with were, to name but a few: a moral life; the political rules a Prince should follow; citizens' right to political resistance; natural and divine law; the contract of the citizens with the sovereign; man's relation to God; love; hate; violence; conditions of war. To the best of my knowledge, philosophers and thinkers were always concerned with improving the quality of political rule, of human life, thus attempting to make the world a more civilized place, a world worthy to live in for everybody, a more just world.

Think about how many interesting and intelligent books and texts had been published before Rousseau's time, from Aristotle's six forms of government to Montaigne's essays to Hobbes' *Leviathan* to Locke's right to resistance and Montesquieu's separation of powers. They all thought about human life, political rule, the rules of a civilization and good and evil and how they could improve mankind's life. None of the various currents of philosophical inquiry advocated that the species should vanish from the earth, on the contrary: philosophers and political thinkers were always interested in making life on earth better for our species, to protect and promote its future.

And then, almost out of the blue, or so many of Rousseau's aristocratic contemporaries must have thought, appears this little nobody from Geneva, the son of a watchmaker, and declares that civilization, everything mankind has achieved so far is bad and must be condemned! On top of his nonsensical musings about the good of nature and the evil of civilization, of the enslaving nature of the capitalist division of labour, this little nobody even wins the first prize of the prestigious Dijon academy in 1751![26]

Indeed, one can reproach Rousseau with hypocrisy, paranoia and selfishness that borders on narcissism.[27] His critics and enemies, first and foremost Voltaire,[28] would argue that he was a hypocrite of the highest order: lecturing

---

[26] A superb biography of Rousseau is Leo Damrosch, *Jean-Jacques Rousseau. Restless Genius* (New York: Mariner Book, 2007).

[27] In my humble opinion, the best source about narcissism, its symptoms, behavioural patterns, and characteristic traits is H. G. Tudor on https://narcsite.com/; accessed 27 November 2022. Tudor's analysis is unprecedented because he explains the narcissistic behaviour and mindset in the finest detail. H. G. Tudor should receive the highest accolade because he has been educating the global public about narcissism, helping many victims to recover from narcissistic abuse and warning the public not to get trapped by narcissists. H. G. Tudor is making the world a better place.

[28] An equally superb biography of Voltaire is Roger Pearson, *Voltaire Almighty. A Life in the Pursuit of Freedom* (London: Bloomsbury, 2006).

the world about how to bring up children in his treatise on education *Emile*, while having rid himself of his own five children, condemning them to a cruel upbringing in orphanages.

Rousseau was selfish to the core—a lot of *cupiditas* with Thérèse Le Vasseur, no *caritas* for his children. He also changed his Calvinist confession when he saw a personal benefit to becoming a Catholic and then returned to Protestantism, again motivated by selfish reasons. The paranoiac way he had accused David Hume (1711–1776) of stealing money from him, after Hume had generously provided him with shelter and food while the Genevan was in England, leaves one speechless.[29] Certainly, one can reproach Rousseau his negative character traits and bad decisions, but one has to admire him for his revolutionary political ideas, his critical questioning of civilization and his promotion of direct democracy. His intellectual audacity, his thoughts were so fresh and bold that he rightfully belongs in the pantheon of great thinkers.

Rousseau added an immensely interesting new theme to philosophy: the idea that nature is good, and man's social order, namely civilization, bad. Rousseau turned the mainstream philosophical thinking of his times on its head: man can be happy and free only if he recognizes the

---

[29] I mustered all my patience, tolerance, understanding and attention to listen to the *Confessions* on Audible. Rousseau does not mention the affair of the money with David Hume. He explains his decision to send away the five children he had with the illiterate Le Vasseur by saying that the institutions would take better care of them than he ever could. Sending them to orphanages would therefore be in their best interest, while he would have the time and quiet to focus on his work.

overpowering beauty and goodness of nature. With regard to political rule, the Genevan praised direct democracy as the only legitimate form of government: if I delegate my right to vote and elect, I have ceased to be a free citizen, and because I have delegated my freedom as a citizen, I have ceased to be alive. If I give up my freedom, I am no longer a human being. From this follows that I am dead, as a citizen, as a human being; I am nothing other than an animal walking on two legs.

Certainly, the survival of *homo sapiens* on our blue planet has been threatened. The last big threat to mankind's survival was the technological possibility of a nuclear war during the years of the Cold War (1948–1991).[30] Yet, during the Cold War, nobody expressed the idea that if a nuclear war extinguished human life on our planet, the planet would be saved. Everybody was afraid, and I think that fear saved mankind; the nuclear balance of power between the USA and the Soviet Union saved mankind from extinguishing itself. Nobody denied or questioned our species' progress and development in individual, political and legal terms.

I hold that today the anti-natalist VHEMT is as revolutionary as Rousseau's critique of civilization was in his times. Therefore, the issue of not having children, of rejecting procreation, is a philosophical question, for all of us to discuss.

---

[30] I define the Cold War as follows: the US Marshall Plan, launched in 1948 was the beginning of the systemic political divide between the West and the Soviet Union, the separation into two ideological camps. The Cold War ended with the political and economic collapse of the Soviet bloc and the dissolution of the Warsaw Pact in 1991.

Second, is an individual's deliberate, hence rational, refusal to create offspring legitimate in ethical and political terms? Yes, I have no doubts that the rejection of procreation is legitimate in ethical and political terms. If I live in a free society, that is, a Western-type democracy and rule-of-law state that grants my civil rights, I have the right not to procreate. Apart from the fact that nobody is interested in my personal decisions, in the way I arrange and manage my life, my decision is legitimate in ethical and political terms since they originate in my free will, in my exercise of my civil rights as a citizen. Just think of the opposite: if my government can pressure me into motherhood against my will, what does that say about the regime?

Europe's political history has examples of regimes that forced motherhood on women. Is it not interesting that authoritarian and totalitarian states have always institutionalized procreation, actively encouraging women to become mothers? Nazi Germany had the *Reich's* mothers producing sons for Goebbel's *Endsieg*, honouring especially fertile women with the *Ehrenkreuz der Deutschen Mutter*, [31] while the Croatian *Ustasha* regime and the Slovak clerical fascist Tiso regime had similar programmes that were intended to guarantee the future of their nations.

A superbly researched question that is related to the theme of deliberate rejection of procreation is Orna Donath's

---

[31] Lebendiges Museum online LeMO on https://www.dhm.de/lemo/kapitel/ns-regime/innenpolitik/mutterkreuz.html; accessed 4 December 2022.

study about regretting motherhood.[32] She has interviewed twenty-three Israeli mothers from all social classes, ethnic backgrounds and religions who have admitted that they regret having had children, although they love them. To them, motherhood is ambivalent: "the co-existence of love and hatred".[33]

To conclude: motherhood is perhaps one of the last taboos of modern society. To some, life is unthinkable without children; to others, life is enjoyable only without children. Should we pass judgement? I think judging individuals on their life choices is everybody's right, as it is just the expression of one's opinion. Motherhood as a choice should never become a political issue, certainly not in a free society. I should always have the freedom to debate anything, but I should not have children if I do not want any.

A modern and tolerant society can deal with diversity of opinion, even if an idea is utopian, promoting the revolutionary idea of mankind's voluntary extinction, the death of our species, *homo sapiens*. Let me conclude with a quote from an immensely gifted modern thinker:

> "Of course social and political collisions will take place; the mere conflict of positive values alone makes this unavoidable. Yet they can, I believe, be minimised by promoting and preserving an uneasy equilibrium, which

---

[32] Orna Donath, "Regretting motherhood: A sociopolitical analysis", *Journal of Women in Culture and Society 40*, no. 2 (2015): 343-367. Donath conducted her study from 2008 to 2011.
[33] Donath quotes the psychologist Rozsika Parker, who coined the concept of maternal ambivalence, Parker, Rozsika (1994). "Maternal Ambivalence". *Winnicott Studies* no 9. 3-17, 10-11.

is constantly threatened and in constant need of repair—that alone, I repeat, is the precondition for decent societies and morally acceptable behaviour, otherwise we are bound to lose our way."[34]

---

[34] Isaiah Berlin, "The Pursuit of the Ideal", in *The Proper Study of Mankind. An Anthology of Essays* (London: Pimlico, 1998),16.

V. Niccolò Machiavelli and the CIA: *Homeland*

Dedicated to the screenwriters of *Hatufim* and the screenwriters of *Homeland*

Introduction

Carrie Mathison: "I am never done!"[1]

This essay is an inquiry into the very successful US TV series *Homeland,* further referred to as HL.[2] I thus deal with fictitious characters and plots. My analysis is interdisciplinary: I combine plot presentation and analysis with aspects of political theory.

We look at Carrie Mathison and her boss Saul Berenson's characters as examples of Machiavellian thinking and agency. Since they are CIA, the principal task of Saul, the director, and Carrie, his best analyst and case officer, is to protect the US from foreign and domestic threats. They cannot afford ethical considerations or moral musings about human and civil rights. They must act to prevent threats and gather information about hostile activities, while running their agents on enemy territory, which involves the coercion, blackmail and sometimes also the sacrifice of an asset to secure an operation that is more important than one human life, because it will save thousands of lives.

---

[1] S1: E3.
[2] Basic information about *HOMELAND* on https://www.imdb.com/title/tt1796960/; accessed 27 November 2021.

Note that to be capable of making these crucial decisions, HL agents use words that de-emotionalize the context, for example 'an operation'. Saul and Carrie speak of their agent as 'our asset', and 'our target', the hostile individual they must 'eliminate', i.e. kill. Thus, if you are CIA and conducting an operation, you act according to plan and finish the job.

Naturally, my assumptions and speculations about how a secret service works, are unprofessional. Why? Because I have no idea how a secret service works—the word 'secret' gives it away.

The US Homeland Security was founded in the aftermath of 9/11.[3] The series HL was inspired by the Israeli series *Hatufim, Prisoners of War,* which ran for two seasons, most probably due to a much smaller budget.[4] *Hatufim* is a superbly written series that addresses a new theme: how do former prisoners of war deal with their lives once they are back home? How do their families cope with a father or a mother who has been in enemy captivity for a longer period of time? How do war veterans come to terms with their PTSD, nightmares, and survivor's guilt?[5]

---

[3] https://www.dhs.gov/topic/homeland-security-enterprise/: accessed 27 November 2021.

[4] https://www.imdb.com/title/tt1676462/; accessed 26 November 2021.

[5] Survivor's guilt is a form of post-traumatic stress disorder PTSD; see https://www.medicalnewstoday.com/articles/325578, accessed 30 November 2021; for an explanation of PTSD see https://www.mayocl inic.org/diseases-conditions/post-traumatic-stress-disorder/sympto ms-causes/syc-20355967; accessed 30 November 2021.

Analysis of threats and terrorist conspiracies is never a simple task, thus best accomplished with rational and pragmatic thought, following the father of political realism Niccolò Machiavelli (1469–1527), the Florentine statesman.[6]

> "All states, all powers, that have held and hold rule over men have been and are either republics or principalities [*sono o repubbliche o principati*]. Principalities are either hereditary, in which the family has been long established; or they are new. […] Such dominions thus acquired are either accustomed to live under a prince, or to live in freedom [*o consueti a vivere sotto un principe, o usi a essere liberi*]; and are acquired either by the arms of the prince himself, or of others, or else by fortune or by ability [*o per fortuna o per virtù*]."[7]

At the beginning of his *Prince*, Machiavelli clearly distinguishes republics from principalities, addressing political freedom, that is liberty, and its opposite, a prince who is ruling in absolute fashion. His thoughts, dedicated to Lorenzo di Piero de' Medici, also referred to as Lorenzo il

---

[6] Sir Isaiah Berlin's analysis of Machiavelli's political thought is the most convincing study to me: "The Originality of Machiavelli", in *The Proper Study of Mankind. An Anthology of Essays* (London: Pimlico, 1998), 269–325. An excellent collection of essays, presenting analysis of such diverse topics as, for example, Machiavelli's influence on Renaissance theatre and a comparison of his *Prince* with Sun Tse's *The Art of War*, is John M. Najemy, ed., *Machiavelli* (Cambridge: Cambridge University Press, 2010).

[7] Niccolò Machiavelli, *The Prince*, Poland 2020, chapter 1, 1. The Italian parts in brackets are from Niccolò Machiavelli, *Il Principe. I Discorsi. Con introduzione e note di Adolfo Oxilia* (Sancasciano Val di Pesa (Firenze) 1935 (8)), first edition 1926, 5.

Magnifico (1449–1492),[8] focus on the absolute rule of a sovereign and what the prince should do and avoid doing to keep his strength[9] over the ruled and the state safe and prospering. Furthermore, he distinguishes domestic affairs and international, or back then on the Italian peninsula in the 16th century, inter-state, or inter-principality relations. Machiavelli identifies dangers to the state in a twofold fashion: they can have their origins at home, hence literally under the prince's nose, or they can loom from the outside,[10] from other states.

Furthermore, Machiavelli does not deal much with republics in his *Prince*, since citizens who enjoy political freedom elect their ruler and are hence as much accountable and responsible for the fate of their republic as the elected ruler. Machiavelli does not say that republics can also be subject to *fortuna*, the fickle moods of the Roman goddess of chance, or that the citizens in a republic can spectacularly fail, for example, by electing a ruler who neglects his tasks, but he does think about the conditions of a republic, ruled by a

---

[8] A brief biography of Lorenzo il Magnifico on https://www.treccani.it/enciclopedia/medici-lorenzo-de-detto-il-magnifico/; accessed 30 January 2022.

[9] Note that I use Hannah Arendt's (1906–1975) definitions of power for a democratically elected government, and strength for a non-democratically elected government or sovereign; therefore, the US government is in power, while Russia's government is in a position of strength over its citizens, and believing Christians of both states respect the authority of their respective national church. Arendt's definitions of power, strength, and authority in *On Violence* (New York: Harvest 1970), 44-46.

[10] Machiavelli, *The Prince*, chapter XIX, 52.

senate or a *concilium* of nobles, and how it faces political adversity.[11]

Machiavelli concentrates on the absolute power of the prince because he witnessed what had happened to states led by weak sovereigns when confronted with stronger enemies. His political thought addresses the strength of an absolute sovereign, while in HL, Saul and Carrie are protecting a republic, a completely different form of government than Florence and the Italian city states in the 15th and 16th centuries.

Yet, is the protection of the state in HL not similar to the suggestions Machiavelli formulated for his Tuscan prince, because the threats are roughly the same, such as threats to the government, the survival and functioning of the state and lastly the protection of the people? Do Carrie and Saul, protecting the American republic, not use secret plans, analysis of the threat situation and positive PR, the very tools Machiavelli suggests to his *Prince*?

Our comparison addresses, first, the issue of *quantity*: with Machiavelli's *Prince*, we have one sovereign. With the US government, we have a democratically elected president with his government as the executive, checked and balanced by both houses as the legislative, and the constitutional court as the judiciary. The American people are the sovereign. About the *quality* of both forms of government: the sovereignty of the Tuscan prince is absolute, while the power of the US government *per se* cannot be absolute since the goal of the American Revolution of 1776 was to get rid of the

---

[11] Machiavelli, *The Prince*, chapter IX, 24-26.

absolutism of the British sovereign ruling his overseas colonies. The wise fathers of the US constitution anticipated threats from the outside and inside, and HL reflects these threats in superb fashion.

I scrutinize HL series 1 to 3, which portrays an external threat exercised by marine sniper Nicholas Brody, an American citizen, thus an insider. Series 8 deals with an internal and an external threat, too: Carrie, an insider, turns into an external threat to the US and the CIA because of her defection to the Russian Federation.

The series begins in 2011, ten years after 9/11. On that day, America, the most generous and democratic nation in the world, a melting pot and new home for all who leave their countries because of political persecution, oppression, and dysfunctional economies, changed for good.

Now, does Machiavellian thought apply to HL? Is Saul, impersonated by Mandy Patinkin, the master and commander, and Carrie, played by Claire Danes, his loyal employee and reliable case officer? Or is it the other way round?

In the first chapter, I present two definitions that will serve as points of orientation for the reader: first, I define "political sustainability", and second, "political efficiency". These definitions will help us better understand the details of the plot and the reasons why Carrie and Saul act and make decisions the way they do. In the following, I present three selected principles of Machiavellian thought, concentrating on the specific instructions for the behaviour of the prince. These principles can be applied to the following *personae* in series 1 to 3 and 8, since they all are at the top level of decision-making with regard to the political survival of their states: Saul, Carrie and Yevgeni Gromov, then Abu Nazir, US President Elizabeth Keane, played by Elizabeth Marvel, and GRU[12] boss Colonel Sergei Mirov, portrayed by Merab Ninidze.

In the second chapter, I present a summary of HL series 1, 2 and 3, followed by a summary of series 8; I thus present the story of Carrie and Brody, portrayed by Damian Lewis, as the beginning of the series, and the end, Carrie living with GRU colonel Yevgeni Gromov in Moscow. Gromov is portrayed by Costa Ronin, who starred in the successful TV series *The Americans*.[13] Note that owing to constraints of space I cannot present a summary of all the subplots, characters, and side plots; such an endeavour would mean writing a book in its own right.

In the conclusion, I shall answer the following research questions: First, who leads, guides and influences whom— does Saul influence Carrie or the other way round? Is it Carrie who explores operative possibilities Saul does not see? Who recognizes a terrorist threat to the US first: Carrie or Saul? Second, is Carrie a convincing example of political sustainability and political efficiency?

---

[12] G.R.U. stands for *Glavnoe Razvedivatel'noe Upravlenie*, Main Intelligence Directorate of the General Staff of the Armed Forces of the Russian Federation, https://simple.wikipedia.org/wiki/GRU; accessed 27 November 2021. About Russia's Army see https://eng.mil.ru/; accessed 27 November 2021.

[13] https://en.wikipedia.org/wiki/The_Americans; accessed 4 February 2022.

I. Definitions and three selected principles of Machiavellian advice

The Oxford English Dictionary OED online defines "sustainability" as first, "the quality of being sustainable by argument; the capacity to be upheld or defended as valid, correct or true; second, the quality of being sustainable at a certain rate or level; and third, the property of being environmentally sustainable".[14]

The Merriam-Webster online dictionary defines "efficiency" as "the ability to do something or produce something without wasting materials, time, or energy: the quality or degree of being efficient".[15]

For the purpose of this paper, I have added the dimension of political decision-making and political activity, both domestic and international. Here are my definitions of "political sustainability" and "political efficiency":

> "Political sustainability is the quality of an individual or a group that keeps their decisions politically sustainable, that is, as valid and correct guidance and consistent continuity in the realm of domestic and international politics in order to protect the state and its government."

> "Political efficiency is a characteristic trait of an individual or a group, who make(s) political decisions and act(s) according to the principle of not wasting time,

---

[14] https://www.oed.com/view/Entry/299890; accessed 28 January 2022.
[15] https://www.merriam-webster.com/dictionary/efficiency; accessed 28 January 2022.

money, personal involvement and individual assets, i.e., personnel or human resources."

Apart from the rather banal statement that the essence of Machiavellianism is to sustain and protect the state with a dispassionate hence rational mind, thus stay in power or hold a position of strength at all levels of decision-making, I find three principles of Machiavellian thought, quoted below, particularly apt to explain the details of the HL plots. Readers should keep these in the back of their minds, as they are quite self-explanatory when applied to the decisions of our HL heroes and villains. Machiavellian thought is not rocket science.

Principle 1: Prudence and humanity—or embodying kindness and stability

> "[…] I say that every prince ought to desire to be considered clement and not cruel. […] Therefore, a prince, so long as he keeps his subjects united and loyal, ought not to mind the reproach of cruelty […] Nevertheless, he [the new prince, add. JB] ought to be slow to believe and to act, nor should he himself show fear, but proceed in a temperate manner with prudence and humanity, so that too much confidence may not make him incautious and too much distrust render him intolerable."[16]

---

[16] Machiavelli, *The Prince*, chapter XVII, 45.

Principle 2: The necessity of appearing to have good qualities—or good PR

> "If men were entirely good this precept would not hold, but because they are bad, and will not keep faith with you, you too are not bound to observe it with them. [...] Therefore, it is unnecessary for a prince to have all the good qualities I have enumerated, but it is very necessary to appear to have them. And I shall dare to say this also, that to have them and always to observe them is injurious, and that to appear to have them is useful; to appear merciful, faithful, humane, religious, upright, and to be so, but with a mind so framed that should you require not to be so, you may be able and know how to change to the opposite."[17]

Principle 3: The avoidance of being hated—or know thy subjects

> "[...] under this generality, that the prince must consider, [...] how to avoid those things which will make him hated or contemptible. It makes him hated above all things, [...] to be rapacious, and to be a violator of the property and women of his subjects, from both of which he must abstain. [...] It makes him contemptible to be considered fickle, frivolous, effeminate, mean-spirited, irresolute [...] and he should endeavour to show in his actions greatness, courage, gravity, and fortitude. [...] And one of the most efficacious remedies that a prince can have against conspiracies [domestic and foreign conspiracies, add. JB] is not to be hated and despised by the people,

---

[17] Machiavelli, *The Prince*, chapter XVIII, 48, 49.

for he who conspires against a prince always expects to please them by his removal; but when the conspirator can only look forward to offending them, he will not have the courage to take such a course, for the difficulties that confront a conspirator are infinite." [18]

II. Summaries of HL series 1 to 3, and series 8

II. 1   The story of Carrie Mathison and Nicholas Brody, series 1 to 3

The pilot S1:E1 begins with the US Delta Force finding a marine held captive in an underground compound in Iraq. At the same time, Carrie Mathison talks to an informant in Bagdad prison, who will be executed shortly. Hoping to evade the execution, he tells her about an American prisoner of war whom al-Qaeda[19] has turned for Abu Nazir.

Ten months later in Washington, D.C.: Carrie is back home from a night with some stranger, cat washes and arrives late for an analyst meeting at the CIA HQ in Langley, Virginia. Marine sergeant Nicholas Brody, a sniper, has been debriefed at Ramstein air base in Germany and meets wife Jessica, son Chris and daughter Dana after eight years of captivity. The family thought him dead long ago, and Jessica has begun a relationship with Brody's best friend Mike Faber, whom the children are very fond of. Carrie suspects Brody to be the turned POW and has her friend Virgil and his brother Max, both technology experts, install listening devices and

---

[18] Machiavelli, *The Prince*, chapter XIX, 52.
[19] https://www.britannica.com/topic/al-Qaeda; accessed 15 December 2021.

cameras in the Brody family home. This is illegal, but she is sure that she is right, and the Piotrowski brothers trust her.

When Brody appears at the CIA HQ, Saul tasks Carrie with his interrogation. What happened to his sniper team colleague, Tom Walker? Brody replies that a guard told him that al-Qaeda members had beaten Walker to death. Unable to sleep, Carrie dresses up and goes to a bar to pick up a man for sex, which is her understanding of intimacy, because she has never been in love. At the bar, she flirts with a man, and it is quite clear that they will engage in sex later. Yet, as Carrie sees how the fingers of a guitarist player on the bar's TV screen move to the rhythm of the music, she remembers Brody moving his fingers in a certain rhythm while being interviewed by several national TV channels. She is certain that the American hero moves his fingers to signal to his handlers that he is ready. She dumps the admirer and rushes to Saul's home, explaining that Brody's fingers display a pattern whenever he is on camera. She convinces Saul that Brody is the turned POW.

Brody has flashbacks, remembering how Abu Nazir forced him to beat Walker to death and then bury him in a shallow desert grave. Saul meets a federal judge whom he blackmails into issuing a warrant to have the Brody house monitored for four weeks. This is a nice little Machiavellian move of Saul's: the judge should not have let himself be captured on camera with a prostitute. Your weakness is my hold over you.

After the four weeks have expired, Carrie's team has to clear Brody's house of the devices, but Carrie is certain that they have missed something. She decides to get close to

Brody and walks into him when he is about to join a veteran support group at his local church. They flirt; he is quite into her, but it is not clear if Carrie is attracted to him too or just pretending.

When the Pakistani secret service abducts terrorist Afsal Hamid from his family home in Islamabad and hands him over to the Americans, CIA director David Estes orders Saul to interrogate Hamid. Carrie suggests to Saul asking Brody about Hamid, he might know him. Brody recognizes Hamid on a video tape; he had guarded him in the compound in Iraq, and once pissed on him. Brody convinces director Estes to let him meet his former torturer, and minutes into their meeting, he physically attacks Hamid. Later, Carrie and Saul learn that Hamid has committed suicide in his cell. Who slipped him the razor blade?

Carrie looks at the video and notices that Brody has drawn Hamid away from the space covered by the camera, so that their fight is not on tape. Carrie sees that which everybody else overlooks; she thinks lightning fast, analyses a situation in seconds, has no pre-formed opinion or bias, is always alert and thinks out of the box. A frustrated Brody calls Carrie, who gave him her card after she had interrogated him. The sniper hero is upset because he has just had a row with marine brother Lauder Wakefield, who had been crippled while serving in Iraq. Lauder has asked Brody about Tom Walker, who was the best sniper in their platoon. How come Walker is dead and Brody alive? Carrie joins Brody in the bar, and they get drunk together; she tells him of Hamid's suicide, seemingly confiding in him. They kiss and have sex in her car.

On a Friday afternoon, Brody and Carrie meet up again at a bar and play billiards when a white supremacist with the infamous 88 tattooed on his arm[20] tries to chat Carrie up; she punches him in the face, and she and Brody escape from the armed gang. They spend the weekend at her family's cabin at the lake, doing what people falling in love do: talk about their teenage years, their dreams, their hardships, cook, drink wine, make love. Brody feels free with Carrie because she understands him, working in a job that is similar to his service in the army, requiring discipline, respect and loyalty. He has nightmares, shouting the name 'Issa', which Carrie, who is a light sleeper, memorizes.

The next morning, Carrie lets slip a remark about Brody's preferred tea, which she noticed while monitoring him weeks ago. Brody is immediately suspicious, and Carrie tells him that she thinks he is an al-Qaeda asset. He denies this, explaining that his moving fingers is a comfort thing he does when under stress. He is a Muslim and has no prayer beads, that's why he moves his fingers. Saul learns from a young American woman arrested as a terrorist that the contact who instructed her and her Saudi boyfriend is Tom Walker. Brody's sniper partner is very much alive and in Washington. Elizabeth Gaines, an influential Party member, invites the Brodys to a dinner party, introducing them to Washington's political elite.

Brody remembers Abu Nazir's eight-year-old son Issa, whom he had taught English, back in Iraq. Issa and eighty-two

---

[20] 88 is a symbol for 'Heil Hitler', see https://www.adl.org/education/references/hate-symbols/88; accessed 13 December 2021.

other children died in a drone bombing targeting Abu Nazir, which Vice President William Walden had authorized. Walden's ethically repugnant argumentation had been that if Abu Nazir hides among children, it is he who kills them, not the US. The drone bomb hit a school, and Abu Nazir and Brody, by then a member of the Nazir family's household, buried Issa together.

Vice President Walden suggests to Brody that he run for congress, aiming to use the American hero for his own political ends, and Brody is flattered by these new and financially beneficial prospects. Carrie's sister Maggie, a physician who has been illegally providing Carrie for years with the medication she needs to keep her CIA employment, reveals Carrie's secret to Saul: "She is bipolar."[21] The Brody family take a trip to Gettysburg in Pennsylvania. Brody explains to his children the details of the decisive battle of the American Civil War.[22] His motives for travelling to Gettysburg are, however, not of an educational nature. With an excuse, Brody slips away from family lunch in a diner and visits a tailor's shop. He puts on a suicide vest and asks the smoking Arab tailor how to operate it.

'On May 19, 2003, Vice President Walden sanctioned the drone bombing of a school in Iraq.' These are Brody's first words on a video he makes to explain and justify his future actions. He hides the camera's chip in the stone wall of a park, marking the hiding place with a sign. The night before

---

[21] S1:E11.
[22] https://www.gettysburgpa.gov/history/slideshows/battle-history; accessed 12 December 2021.

Walden's speech in front of the Capitol to announce his intention of running for president, Walker kidnaps an elderly lady, from whose apartment he has a clear shot at the Capitol. Carrie thinks that something is going to happen, that they are missing something; she meets Virgil in front of the Capitol. From the elderly lady's apartment, Walker shoots Elizabeth Gaines, upon which the Secret Service rushes Walden, Brody, and everybody in front of the Capitol down to the bunker, ignoring security protocols. In the bunker, Brody activates the suicide vest, but it does not explode; one might cynically speak of a 'wardrobe malfunction.'[23] Carrie frantically drives to the Brody's family home and implores daughter Dana to call her dad. Dana begs Brody to come home, and he obliges.

Series 1 ends with Brody meeting Walker in a tunnel; it is dark, wet, and cold. Walker is marine 2 and Brody marine 1 in Abu Nazir's revenge plan to kill Walden. With physical and psychological torture, both marines have been turned while in al-Qaeda captivity. Walker reproaches Brody that he has not followed Abu Nazir's plan. Walker's task was to just shoot somebody close to Walden, causing the Secret Service to rush the politicians down to the bunker, where Brody would then kill them all by detonating his suicide vest. On Abu

---

[23] The euphemistic expression 'wardrobe malfunction' emerged in the aftermath of the Super Bowl XXXVIII in 2004: it served as an excuse for Justin Timberlake to rip off Janet Jackson's jacket during their performance, which exposed one of her nipples—a true scandal, since children were watching! Half of the country rolled on the floor laughing at the explanation, while the other half believed it. Details on https://en.wikipedia.org/wiki/Super_Bowl_XXXVIII_halftime_show_controversy; accessed 30 January 2022.

Nazir's command, Walker hands the phone over to Brody, and Abu Nazir understands why Brody did not activate the vest: it is much more efficient to kill an idea, than a man, and with Brody as a future congressman and confidant of Walden, he can change US policy towards al-Qaeda. Brody has thus lied to Abu Nazir, omitting the fact that the vest did not explode. Presenting himself as a resourceful ally, Brody convinces Abu Nazir to keep him on. Abu Nazir issues a command, and Brody shoots Walker; this is one of Abu Nazir's many Machiavellian decisions, since Walker has done his deed and knows too much. It is simply too dangerous to keep him alive.

Series 2 begins a few months after Israel's bombing of Iran's nuclear factories. We see Carrie working as an English teacher in a school for immigrants. Unbeknownst to everybody, save for Carrie who cannot believe that she was wrong, Brody is active for Abu Nazir; his main contact is Palestinian journalist Roya, an attractive brunette who speaks with a posh British accent.

A woman in Beirut called Fatima contacts Saul, warning him of an imminent attack, but she wants to speak only to Carrie, who has recruited her years ago. Fatima is the wife of a Hezbollah leader, who physically abuses her; she wants to get out of the marriage and move to the US. Saul thus needs Carrie's help, and after a few days of reflection, she flies to Cyprus and takes on a cover identity.

In Beirut, Carrie enjoys the dangerous game of cat and mouse. Chased by Lebanese security officers, she escapes through a bazaar, and we see her happily grinning. She loves the excitement and the danger. From Fatima, whom she meets in a mosque after the service, Carrie learns that Abu Nazir will meet Fatima's husband in Beirut in a few days. The CIA sets up an operation to have Abu Nazir and the Hezbollah leader killed by snipers. When Abu Nazir and his heavily armed entourage arrive in Beirut, Brody is in the situation room following the operation with Vice President Walden and top US government and military officials. He sends Abu Nazir a warning text, and the terrorist escapes at the last second. Carrie, Fatima, Saul, and a male CIA operative are about to leave in an SUV, which an angry mob is physically attacking, but Carrie reasons that there must be some source material or documentation belonging to Fatima's husband in their flat. She rushes up to the apartment and grabs a bag and some papers. Several nerve-racking minutes later, she escapes from a male mob, makes it back down to the SUV, and the team leaves. But the immense risk she has put the team and herself through is worth it: in the bag, Saul finds a USB stick with the video Brody had made before the Capitol shooting, proof of his treason.

After the debriefing at CIA HQ, Carrie is in her apartment, lonely and suicidal since the CIA has not reinstated her. So desperate is she that she drinks white wine and swallows a lot of sleeping pills, but her stomach cannot take them. Her doorbell rings: it is Saul, straight from the airport. He shows her Brody's video, and Carrie is in tears of relief: "I was right!"[24]

Since Saul has Brody's video to prove that he is a traitor and a terrorist, CIA director Estes gives the green light for a

---

[24] S2:E3.

new operation: keeping Brody under surveillance. Carrie is reinstated, joins the team in the safe house and meets new operative Peter Quinn, portrayed by Rupert Friend.

The team's next step is to let Brody know that Carrie is back at the CIA, to lure him into action and make him reveal his contacts. On his way to the HQ, Brody spots Carrie walking out of the building; they exchange a few friendly words, and Brody informs Roya that Carrie is back at the CIA. Lonely Brody drinks at a Washington hotel bar; he has left the family home. He calls Carrie, and they have a drink and a chat. She later shows up in front of his hotel room, provoking him with the information about his video. The CIA barges in and arrests Brody. As head of the operation, Quinn plans the interrogation.

Quinn is loyal to Dar Adal, portrayed by F. Murray Abraham; Adal is a black operations specialist and an old acquaintance of Saul's. A few minutes into the interrogation, Quinn suddenly drives a knife through Brody's hand, inflicting physical pain to make him psychologically vulnerable. Immediately, operatives drag Quinn out of the interrogation room—now, it's Carrie's moment. She plays the good cop, the friendly and understanding interrogator; this is part two of Quinn's plan. Appealing to Brody's sense of honour as a marine and their past relationship, she tells him that deep down she knows he is a good man, a decent and honourable man. Switching off the cameras is a further sign that he can trust her, a clever move by her, designed to soften him up. After just a few minutes, Carrie breaks Brody: if he tells them everything about Abu Nazir now, the CIA won't press charges. There won't be a trial, no noisy press occupying the family's front lawn, and he can walk out today as a free man and a CIA employee, on top of that. Carrie thus makes Brody a rational offer he cannot refuse. This is not a Machiavellian offer, since the Florentinian would most probably suggest eliminating Brody, who is a traitor and therefore cannot be trusted. But Carrie sees his potential, recruits him, turning him into one of theirs, thus offering Brody a way out from the hold Abu Nazir has over him. She drives him home, and when wife Jessica asks him to end the secrecy and lies for good, Brody replies that he is working for the CIA.

Since the CIA knows about the Gettysburg tailor, they send Quinn and a forensic team to the shop, where four men in black uniforms attack them. Then, the attackers break down a wall in the shop and get out some heavy weaponry. Quinn, shot and feigning death, sees them leave with the weapons.

Instructed by Saul and Carrie, Brody tells Roya that he is quitting; this puts Abu Nazir, who has arrived in Washington, under pressure of time. The Iraqi hides in a defunct factory, and once his gang have kidnapped Carrie, he has Brody at his beck and call. Carrie's life for Walden's—that is the deal. Abu Nazir tells Brody to get the number of Walden's pacemaker in exchange for Carrie's life. Brody finds the number in Walden's office, frantically texts it to Abu Nazir, and he lets Carrie go. When Walden enters his office, he has heart problems; Abu Nazir's guys have stopped the pacemaker electronically, and Walden dies. Brody watches him die and tells him about Issa, whom he loved like his own son. This is Brody and Abu Nazir's revenge for the bombing of the Iraqi school.

Carrie suspects that Abu Nazir is still hiding in the factory compound. Why? After showering Carrie with obscene words, arrogant and stupid Roya tells Carrie in the interrogation room that Abu Nazir would never run. Unlike others, Carrie takes this information verbally and seriously, and on her command, the FBI starts a fresh search of the compound. She is right again: when the police officers find him, Abu Nazir commits suicide by cop.[25]

Carrie and Brody spend some days at the cabin at the lake and talk about their future together. By now, it is clear that Carrie is as much in love with Brody as he is with her. Top CIA officials and some two hundred of Washington's political elite gather for Walden's funeral. It is held at the CIA HQ in Langley because he is a former director of the organization. Carrie and Brody leave the commemoration hall and go up to her office to have an amorous encounter. Looking out of the window, Brody notices that his car has been moved close to the entrance of the building—wham! A huge explosion destroys the lower parts of the building. Brody convinces Carrie that he did not place the bomb, which has killed Cynthia Walden and her teenage son Finn, director Estes and most of the persons attending the funeral. With Carrie's help, Brody flees to Canada. Abu Nazir's weapons from the tailor's shop were a diversion; he had his men place the bomb in Brody's car because he anticipated Walden's funeral would be held at Langley. Abu Nazir has killed more than two hundred people and outwitted the CIA, his principal enemy.

---

[25] https://www.ojp.gov/ncjrs/virtual-library/abstracts/suicide-cop; accessed 19 December 2021.

Series 3 starts with Saul as the new CIA director. He puts a bounty of USD 10 million on Brody's head. Carrie is off her medication, and, after having physically attacked Saul and colleagues at a restaurant, making their lunch an unforgettable experience, she is in psychiatric detention. The CIA have sacked her, and her professional reputation is zero since she has helped traitor and terrorist Brody escape. Her bank account is frozen, her car impounded, and nobody trusts her. She is a pariah in Washington. A lawyer called Bennet offers her a job; she accepts. Her people have forsaken her, but to Iran's secret service, she is an asset. Carrie shows up at Saul's house at night after making sure she is not followed. They have made contact. The operation is on.

Saul's plan is to turn Major General Majid Javadi, the head of Iran's secret service, into a long-term CIA asset, to change Iran's nuclear policy. Farah, member of an Iranian oppositional family and financial specialist, finds evidence that Javadi has transferred millions of dollars from the Revolutionary Guards' accounts to his accounts abroad. Carrie is the bait, and Javadi has taken it. Blackmailed into cooperation with the CIA, greedy and ruthless Javadi sticks to Saul's deal, but hastens to slaughter his ex-wife and daughter-in law in a brutal attack at their Washington home. I think Javadi killed the women to demonstrate to Saul and himself that he is still an independent operator—which, of course, he is not anymore. Therefore, this is not a Machiavellian move, since not related to the state, but to Javadi's personal frustration, mobilizing him to do something to get even with Saul. It is a cruel act of bravado, since he is painfully aware that he has lost out to Saul, an American Jew, hence a twofold arch enemy.

In the meantime, Brody has made it to South America. A band of Columbian drug dealers, blissfully unaware of the price Saul has put on Brody's head, since they consume their own product, sell the American to a Venezuelan crime gang. The gang holds him captive in a Caracas slum, in a decrepit and unfinished high building referred to as the 'Tower of David'.[26] The gay and paedophile physician on the gang's payroll hooks Brody up on heroin, so that he can't flee. By the time Saul arrives in the slum to hand over the bounty, Brody is a junkie. Saul's team bring him back home to the US, and he slowly recovers with medical care and physical training.

If Saul's plan to turn Javadi into a CIA asset is the first phase of his plan, the second phase is to have Brody eliminate Danesh Akbari, the current leader of the Revolutionary Guards. With Akbari dead, Javadi will become the leader of the Revolutionary Guards, the most powerful man in Iran, and hence under Saul's control. The logical beauty of this plan is perfect, a Machiavellian plan. Also because of his feelings for Carrie, Brody is eager to prove his loyalty to the CIA and begin the operation; he is back to his former fitness and has a clear mind.

The CIA gets Brody across the Iraq-Iran border at immense human cost, and Javadi brings him to Teheran. When US marine sniper Nicholas Brody, a Muslim, and confidant of the murdered hero Abu Nazir asks Iran for political asylum, condemning the US as a devilish state, he is

---

[26] S2: E3.

a star on Iranian national TV. Brody meets Abu Nazir's widow, who has found refuge in Iran and is close to Akbari. She arranges a meeting. Carrie is in Teheran to organize the extraction of Brody and herself.

Brody meets Akbari in his office and tells him how grateful he is for the political asylum. Then, he asks Akbari about Abu Nazir. It all started here in this office, Akbari replies. In that moment, something in Brody's mind snaps and he kills Akbari with an ash tray, hides the body behind the desk and walks out of the heavily guarded building. After he has rid himself of the syringe with poison, which was the original plan, Carrie picks him up, and they drive to a farm, waiting for the marines to extract them. In the quiet of the night, Carrie tells Brody that she is expecting his child, and they are happy, looking forward to a future together at home. When the Revolutionary Guards raid the building and arrest Brody, Carrie immediately knows that somebody in the US has betrayed them. Who?

Andrew Lockhart, an ambitious senator shortlisted to become the next CIA director, and Dar Adal have betrayed the extraction plan to Javadi, who is now the leader of the Revolutionary Guards. If their betrayal of Brody is a Machiavellian decision, they pursue two goals: first, to damage Saul's reputation, hence prevent him ever being reappointed CIA director, and second, to eliminate the traitor Brody, whom Saul has hired as an agent. Back in her hotel, Carrie meets Javadi, who tells her that a military tribunal has sentenced Brody to death. The public hanging is scheduled for 4 am. Carrie calls Brody in prison; he is at peace, accepts his fate and wants to die. Carrie and Farah's uncle, her contact in Teheran, attend the execution. In a heart-breaking scene, Carrie, visibly pregnant, watches Akbari's widow put the noose around Brody's neck and spit into his face. A huge crane[27] lifts him up, and Carrie's face is the last thing dying Brody sees.

The story of Carrie and Brody ends at the CIA headquarters four months later: Lockhart is the new CIA director. He vehemently refuses Carrie's demand to honour Brody with a star on the wall of fallen CIA heroes. With Javadi in power, Iran's nuclear policy has changed: international experts now have access to Iran's nuclear factories, which is proof that Saul's plan is working, that Javadi is politically sustainable and efficient. After a commemoration for fallen

---

[27] My friend Jabbar Moradi, an Iranian citizen of Kurdish extraction, explains the particularity of hanging by crane: "The choice of a crane for execution sounds to me an unfortunate coincidence of technology and a barbaric action still in practice, and nothing more. I would say the fact that the regime wants to make a show out of the execution (they perform some public ones; and the non-public ones are so hidden that often the news comes out only days after the execution) is not unique or new, nor is the practice limited to this country. There is a culture surrounding public executions. A lot of people gather to watch, some even take their kids and grab a snack or two! The government often announces the date of the execution and who the condemned criminal is. Mostly, they claim the culprit is a serial killer or rapist or something similar to trigger more interest in seeing justice done. I can imagine since more people are around, a higher more visible spot can be provided by the crane rather than a normal execution stand." E-mail conversation with Moradi on 21 December 2021. Israeli spy Eli Cohen (1924–1965), who had infiltrated the highest echelons of Syria's government, was also executed by public hanging, though not from a crane, as shown in the Netflix film *The Spy*; https://www.britannica.com/biography/Eli-Cohen; accessed 21 December 2021.

CIA heroes, the ceremonial hall is dark, and everybody has left. With a felt-tip pen, lonely Carrie draws a star for Brody on the wall, honouring his sacrifice.

II. 2 Carrie's defection, series 8

Is Carrie a traitor? Why did she defect to Russia? At the beginning of the final season, series 8, we see Carrie recovering. After the GRU has exchanged her for two Russian agents the CIA had captured, she is in a Washington psychiatric ward, healing slowly and getting physically fit.

After her capture in Moscow at the end of series 7, Yevgeni Gromov had stopped her medication because she had refused to make an official statement that Russia was not involved in the murder of general Jamie McClendon, whom GRU captain Simone Martin, the on-and-off girlfriend of White House chief of staff David Wellington, had had poisoned in prison to make US President Elizabeth Keane the main suspect. Paranoiac Keane had hundreds of Washington's administrative personnel and politicians in all institutions arrested after she barely escaped an attempt at her life. Her enemies had referred to her presidency as fascist, and she had been further dividing the country, trying to oppress any criticism of her decisions. The GRU's plot was to use the growing hatred of Keane to Russia's advantage: an unpopular US president having issued the order to have a very popular US general killed in prison would prompt further civil unrest, thus further weaken the US from within. This Russian plan is a superb example of applied

Machiavellianism, beautiful in its perfectly rounded logic. Your democracy is weak because of your First Amendment, which allows me to manipulate public opinion against your president.

The GRU's plan almost succeeds, but Yevgeni underestimates Simone Martin's emotional hurt on learning that his feelings for her are fake, just a show to recruit her for the GRU and have her kill General McLendon. Here, we see what British author Graham Greene (1904–1991) so aptly called *The Human Factor*:[28] Simone Martin's disappointed love for Yevgeni. Love is a human factor, since feelings make actions unpredictable. If I am driven by hatred, love, envy or contempt, my actions will prompt different results or outcomes, and it is impossible for other individuals to predict how I will act and what I will decide.

It was Carrie, who used Yevgeni's devious move with perfect logic, telling Martin that she was in a relationship with Yevgeni. Carrie's little Machiavellian lie, that Yevgeni was just using Martin for his own goals, prompted Martin's defection from the GRU to the CIA. Carrie sacrificed herself when she had the Russian authorities arrest her so that Saul and the team with Martin could fly out of Moscow. Her loyalty, quick thinking and steely willingness to see an operation through have no limits.

US President Keane, blinded by her arrogance, lack of humility and paranoia, has brought the US to the brink of civil war, posing an internal threat to the US constitution. Yet, as

---

[28] https://www.goodreads.com/book/show/62851.The_Human_Factor; accessed 30 January 2022.

unpopular and even hated by some citizens as she is, she eventually does have the grace, patriotism and insight to step down and help the country heal with a new president. Her Vice President Ralph Warner from the other party follows her into office.

Carrie has flashbacks and nightmares, incapable of telling reality apart from delusions. As she has been in Russian detention for 213 days without her medication, the CIA naturally mistrust her; the Russians might have turned her. She fails the polygraph test. In the meantime, Saul oversees the peace negotiations of the Afghan government with the Taliban in Doha, Qatar. Max is with a platoon at the Afghan-Pakistan border to install a listening device, and Saul needs Carrie in Kabul because of her contacts and expertise.

When Carrie waits in front of Afghan Vice-President Abdul Qadir G'ulom's office, she sees Yevgeni and his GRU chums walking out. Back at the Kabul CIA station, she receives an anonymous note with the name of Samira Noori on it. G'ulom had had Samira's husband, a journalist, killed because he had criticized G'ulom's regime. Carrie and her team go through Samira's apartment, and she wonders: why is there a burka hanging in Samira's wardrobe? Samira is a modern educated Afghan woman; why would she have a burka, a symbol of the Taliban's stone-age ideology?

Again, Carrie's out-of-the-box thinking and talent for psychological assessment are spot on; she sees what nobody else sees. She finds a USB stick sewn into the burka. The stick has evidence of G'ulom's corruption racket: he has billed the US millions of dollars for the building of an army base in Afghanistan and a modern Afghan army, both of which exist only on paper. The CIA now has leverage on G'ulom to make him support the peace talks, Saul's Doha Framework.

Saul is in Pakistan to meet Haissam Haqqani, leader of the Taliban. He senses that Haqqani wants peace too and offers him a meeting to talk. Too much blood has been shed on both sides. Haqqani's son Jalal, envious of his father's power, works for the Pakistani secret service, headed by Tasneem Qureishi, who is as beautiful and ruthless as she is ambitious and patriotic. Envious son Jalal betrays Saul and Haqqani's meeting to Tasmeen, and Haqqani barely survives a Pakistani bomb attack on his convoy when on his way to meet Saul. Haqqani's Taliban kidnap Saul. Haqqani listens in on his son's mobile and learns about his betrayal to the Pakistanis. When Jalal shows up, his father throws him out into the streets like a dog. Tasneem and her men pick him up, and Haqqani releases Saul. He trusts him.

Wherever Carrie goes, Yevgeni does not seem to be far away. In an underground expat bar, where she is having a drink with her CIA colleagues, he tells her that it was he who gave her the contact to Samira Noori. A few days later, they meet up on a square, heavily monitored by CIA station chief Mike Dunn and Jenna, a field agent. Carrie doesn't know that her own people are observing her every move. When Yevgeni shows up, they can't hear a thing because the Muezzin has just begun his prayer on the loudspeakers above the square. The GRU is meticulous when planning a simple meeting. Yevgeni tells Carrie that he had saved her life back in Moscow; she had hanged herself in her cell, and he had stormed in at the last minute. Is Yevgeni trying to recruit Carrie for the GRU or is he in love with her? Probably both.

Carrie suggests to US President Warner, portrayed by Beau Bridges, to visit Kabul to support the Doha Framework with his authority and power, even more so as the US plans a withdrawal of their troops, once the Doha Framework is in place.

On her way to Bagram airport, Carrie receives a desperate call from Samira: her Taliban brother-in-law and his cronies are about to abduct her to her native village. He will force her into marriage, as, according to the law, a brother has to take care of the widow of his brother. We see again how courageous Carrie is when a human life is at stake. She commands the driver to rush to Samira's house. When the Taliban frogmarch Samira, whom they have put in a burka, towards their car, Carrie and her team have already sabotaged the car, then threaten them with their superior weapons. Carrie pulls Samira into their SUV, and they leave. Samira is safe.

President Warner lands in Bagram airport, and Carrie welcomes him. He expresses his gratitude because, thanks to her, Simone Martin had spoken out in a hearing, revealing the GRU as the culprits in the murder of General McLendon. Warner and his bodyguards get on a helicopter, referred to as Chalk 1; Afghan President Daoud flies out in Chalk 2. The presidents meet at a US base in the mountains, and Warner tells the troops that they are going home soon. Everybody is happy. Max is supposed to fly out with the President's entourage, but he changes his mind at the last minute. Slightly autistic and shy, Max enjoys the camaraderie with the soldiers, having friends.

Both helicopters crash on their way back to Bagram airbase, and everybody is dead. Have the Taliban shot down the choppers to sabotage the Doha Framework? G'ulom and Tasmeen opposed the Doha Framework from the beginning, G'ulom because he once and for all wants to liquidate the Taliban, and Tasmeen because she does not want the US to interfere in Pakistan's sovereignty. G'ulom, who is President of Afghanistan now, uses the situation to declare martial law, blaming the Taliban for the murder of both presidents. He orders his troops to arrest any Taliban they catch and intern them in Kabul's football stadium.

In the meantime, Carrie scrutinizes the helicopter flight records at Bagram airbase and finds out that the army regularly switches helicopters; she thinks the choppers have crashed because of mechanical failure. She calls Max and asks him to get the black box of the President's helicopter, because they need evidence to save the Doha Framework. Max, protected by four marines, finds it, but a platoon of Taliban attacks them; all four soldiers die, and Max is abducted by a Taliban, who later peddles the black box to a bazaar, unaware what it is.

Carrie is desperate; she hasn't heard from Max since he has confirmed to have found the black box. She asks Yevgeni for help, and the GRU locates the village where Max is held captive. Carrie is supposed to travel to Germany on Saul's command, and Jenna, who admires her, escorts her to the gate, but Carrie escapes and Yevgeni picks her up.

They drive to the village, where Max is held and pay for his life, but Jalal and his cronies show up. Jalal threatens to shoot Max if his father is executed. Haqqani has turned himself in to G'ulom's government because Saul has promised that he and Tasmeen have found a judge who will acknowledge his innocence. But minutes before the trial, the court switches judges, most probably at G'ulom's behest. In a rushed trial that is a mockery of correct judicial procedure in a rule-of-law state, the court sentences Haqqani to death within minutes of the trial opening. G'ulom's troops execute him. Jalal shoots Max to avenge his father, which is what his Taliban cronies expect him to do as a respectful son.

When Carrie and Yevgeni finally find the flight recorder, she pays up and has a brief look at its content before Yevgeni drives a needle with a sedative into her neck and sets off with the black box. New US President Benjamin Hayes is a weakling, hesitating to have the site of the crashed helicopters bombed to pre-empt the Taliban parading dead President Warner's body on social media. Hayes has also hired John Zabel as his foreign policy advisor. Zabel has never served a day in the army but loves to show muscle, especially since a journalist friend has sent him a clip in which Jalal claims at a Taliban meeting that it was he who shot down the choppers. Jajal lies, because he has to strengthen his position as the new leader of the Taliban. While his father wanted to make peace, the Taliban will never give up fighting the Satan USA under Jalal's leadership. Jalal is a war monger, feeding his malicious ego by sowing hatred and violence. Zabel advises President Hayes to bomb the site of the crashed choppers and then threaten Pakistan with war if they do not hand over Jalal within 48 hours. In this highly sensitive atmosphere in such a volatile region, the world is but days away from a nuclear war.

Carrie, back in Washington, informs Saul that in the few minutes she had to inspect the black box before Yevgeni sedated her, she found evidence that the helicopters crashed because of technical failure. Yevgeni is willing to hand over the black box to the US, if Carrie reveals the identity of a CIA asset at the top level of Russia's government. Tit for tat.[29] Saul denies that such a spy exists, but Carrie does not believe him. She is sure that Saul is hiding his deepest secret from her until the moment she needs to know, and she takes over from him—when Saul is dead. The time Yevgeni has given her to identify the spy has run out. Yevgeni instructs Carrie in a video that if she cannot find Saul's spy, she has to kill him. Tit for tat: Saul's life for the black box, and no nuclear war.

This GRU plan is perfectly logical and Machiavellianism in practise: the liquidation of a threat to ensure the sustainability of the state. Saul's death will automatically deactivate his spy in Moscow since a dead Saul can no longer issue instructions and receive information from his asset. Carrie wants the black box to prove that the presidents died in a crash caused by technical failure; the black box is the evidence she needs to convince President Hayes of Haqqani's innocence, to save the Doha Framework and avoid a nuclear war.

Yet, as long as Russia has the black box, Carrie has either to identify Saul's spy or kill him or watch helplessly as the US enters into a nuclear war with Pakistan. Machiavellian

---

[29] An explanation of tit for tat can be found on https://grammarist.com/idiom/tit-for-tat/#:~:text=The%20phrase%20tit%20for%20tat,tap%20is%20hit%2C%20light%20touch; accessed 22 February 2022.

thought is based on the rational analysis of the facts, logical thinking and focussed on the principal goal: to hold on to political power or a position of strength[30] at all costs, while pre-emptively inflicting the highest damage on the enemy, in the rational expectation and empirical knowledge that the enemy will do exactly the same.

Field agent Jenna, who considers leaving the CIA after she has witnessed Jalal's bombing of a bus with US Special Forces at the Pakistan-Afghan border, helps Carrie: in the CIA library, Jenna finds an old asset of Saul's. Young Saul, stationed in East Berlin from 1982 to 1987, had brought GRU officer Andrei Kuznetsov through the East German border minefields to West Berlin in 1987. Carrie visits the Russian in his house in the countryside, presenting herself as a CIA historian, and Kuznetsov shows her a photo of his English teacher and the platoon he fought with. He tells her that Saul used to communicate with him by means of books bound in red leather. Carrie is staying at Saul's house, and looking at his library, she sees a lot of red leather-bound books. Scrutinizing the books, she uncovers all CIA operations Saul's asset was involved in. She finds out that the Russian spy hides his messages in the books' bindings and sends the volumes to an antiquarian bookshop in Washington, addressed to a Professor Rabinov.

Saul is in New York; the UN Security Council is desperately trying to negotiate between the parties. Saul knows Carrie: he is certain that it is only a matter of time

---

[30] See footnote 9 for my usage of Arendt's definitions of power and strength.

before she finds out the identity of his asset. He warns his spy, Anna Pomerantsova, the GRU's chief translator. In 1986, young, attractive and blonde Anna had been an English teacher at the GRU in East Berlin, and after her entire class had been executed following Kuznetsov's defection, she had turned against her government. Saul had hired her, after Anna had shot two GRU agents who had been about to arrest Saul. She had saved his life, proving that he could trust her.

Carrie has identified Anna from Kuznetsov's picture, which is again proof of her out-of-the-box thinking: her rational way of combining facts and her ability to understand a context with all its seemingly independent variables. She asks Saul to admit that Anna is his secret asset, but Saul refuses. When Carrie pleads with him to avoid the impending nuclear war, Saul dryly tells her the war is a regional one. The safety of his Moscow asset is more important. Carrie does not tell Yevgeni about Anna; she needs evidence. She promises Yevgeni to kill Saul, but she also tells him that she has a plan B. If Saul does not reveal the identity of his spy, there is a way of finding out. Yevgeni's men are about to poison Saul, when Carrie aborts the operation, telling them to wait. This is proof of Yevgeni's trust in her: he lets her command his agents, hence lead the operation, certain that she will deliver. He is patient.

Carrie visits Saul's sister Dorit, who lives in Gush Etzion on the Israeli West Bank and tells her that Saul has died of a heart attack. That is a Machiavellian lie to achieve what she needs—information. Dorit packs a suitcase to travel to the funeral in Washington and gives Carrie an envelope Saul has left for her. It is a USB stick: in his video, Saul reveals the identity of his most secret asset in Russia.

Carrie shows Yevgeni, who rushes into Dorit's house, Saul's video. This is the evidence Yevgeni needs. He informs his boss, GRU colonel Mirov, via text message. Colonel Mirov at the UN in New York is truly shocked: his confidant and employee, who could be his mother and whom he tenderly addresses with Anitchka, is a traitor. After a few seconds, he goes after her with his agents. Warned by Saul, Scott Ryan, a confidant of Saul's, and Anna flee to the basement, the Russian agents chasing them. They are trapped: the Russians are about to break in the door, and Anna asks Scott to give her his gun. He refuses, but Anna calls Saul, and Scott eventually obeys Saul who orders him to hand Anna his gun. She shoots herself, with Saul witnessing her suicide on the phone. She has been loyal to him until the last second of her life.

Sitting on Dorit's porch and watching some cute little Israeli boys playing football, Carrie is desperate. Football is a strategic game: lose or win. Yevgeni receives a text from Mirov that Anna has killed herself. He tells Carrie. Thus, Anna is not on the way to the infamous Lubyanka,[31] as desperate Carrie had thought just a few minutes ago. Anna's suicide changes everything, and in a few seconds, Carrie hatches a plan. She and Yevgeni rush to Ramallah, a Russian controlled airbase on Palestinian territory. Since Israel is CIA territory,

---

[31] The current Russian government advertises its totalitarian past in a truly Capitalist fashion: https://www.visitrussia.org.uk/blog/lubyanka-home-of-the-infamous-kgb/; accessed 5 February 2022.

due to the alliance between the US and Israel, they must get out quickly to avoid Carrie's arrest. In the eyes of the CIA, Carrie is now a traitor and defector. If caught, she would have her last meal in a US high security prison.

It is a truly great day for the peace-loving Russian nation, and a field day for the GRU at that. At the press conference set up by the UN delegation of the Russian Federation, Colonel Mirov presents to the global public the analysis of the black box. The presidents died in an accident caused by mechanical failure. He asks US president Hayes to stop the aggression against Pakistan, as the black box proves that Haqqani, his son Jalal and the Taliban are innocent. In Machiavellian terms, the Russian press conference is a clever, rational, and legitimate move. Why?

Yevgeni's deal with Carrie was to exchange the black box for the identity of the CIA asset. Once Mirov has learned that Anna is Saul's asset, the deal would prompt him to hand over the black box to the US. Yet, as Anna has committed suicide, the GRU cannot interrogate her anymore. Therefore, the GRU-CIA deal is null and void, and Russia is no longer obliged to hand over the black box to the US. On the contrary: Russia uses her analysis of the black box for a striking PR stunt.

Colonel Mirov, a convincing actor who displays deep concern for world peace, asks US President Hayes to turn round his jet fighters. Furthermore, at this point in time neither Carrie nor Saul has any leverage over Russia. Moscow is thus completely free to act as she pleases, that is, to realize her own interests in the chess game called global politics.

Chess is an achievement of civilization; it obeys the rules of logical thinking, personal accountability and, at the end of the day, trust. If I play chess, I trust that my adversary sticks to the same rules as I do: we agree on the procedure. Chess is the victory of civilization over the law of the jungle, or the state of nature, a condition Thomas Hobbes (1588–1679) so aptly defined as "the war of every man against every man".[32] Russia is therefore not a rogue actor; she keeps to the rules of chess. Her future actions are predictable, because they follow unimpassioned logic, and, with regard to nuclear power, the logic of the global balance of power. Apart from the fact that the Russian Federation is not a democracy, which to the US government is a major caveat, Russia acts according to the civilizing rules of chess, that is, the strength she has in the UN Security Council and the loyalty and support of her allies.

Colonel Mirov's press conference makes Russia look peace-loving and everybody else stupid and incompetent, killing three birds with one stone. In front of the global audience, the US appears as a war monger, and Mirov is right, considering the facts. You dumb cowboys, don't you do regular maintenance checks on your helicopters? Don't you stupid cattle herders keep up a strict regime of servicing your aircraft? Mirov does not say this explicitly, but that is what he insinuates. Furthermore, Russia identifies Afghan President G'ulom and Taliban leader Jalal, again between the lines, as liars, while the Pakistani government, Russia's ally, looks like an innocent victim, pushed into a nuclear war by the almighty US. Wellington and Saul are relieved, and

---

[32] Thomas Hobbes, *Leviathan,* ed. by Richard Tuck, 2nd revised student edition (Cambridge: Cambridge University Press, 1996), 90.

President Hayes and Zabel have to call back the troops, which is humiliating to the core. In global politics, chess, and football: USA vs. Russian Federation = 0-1.

Two years later: a beautiful summer night in Moscow. We see a splendidly lit Kremlin and the River Moskva from Yevgeni's gorgeous apartment in Moscow's city centre. Carrie is putting on mascara, preparing to go out. Yevgeni, the perfect Russian gentleman and visibly in love with her, compliments her on her looks and gives her a beautiful necklace as a gift for her achievement. What is that achievement, one wonders?

Carrie goes to her office and looks at the wall with her notes. She has written a book about CIA operations, using her name and picture on the cover. This book is an act of high treason. She has dedicated it to her daughter Franny, a redhead like her father Nicholas Brody. Franny lives with Carrie's sister Maggie and her family in Washington, because in series 7, Carrie had accepted the fact that she is incapable of taking care of her child, because of her bi-polar condition and her CIA profession. In psychological and organizational terms, Carrie is not fit to be a mother and she knows it.

She and Yevgeni attend a concert of black US jazz musicians. Carrie excuses herself and goes to the washroom, where a beautiful brunette, who looks like an older Jenna with a lot of make-up, is powdering her nose. The brunette's handbag looks exactly like Carrie's. Carrie picks up the brunette's handbag, and the brunette Carrie's. How has Carrie, constantly observed by the GRU, managed to make contact with the CIA station in Moscow? We shall never find out.

Saul and sister Dorit are clearing out his house in Washington, when he receives a package, addressed to Professor Rabinov. It is *Tyranny of Secrets*—Carrie's book. Saul is astonished, but a gut feeling makes him scrutinize the book's binding—and there, he finds Carrie's message: "Greetings from Moscow, professor. The Russian defence system …"[33] Saul grins, happy to learn that Carrie is now his new asset at the almighty core of the GRU. She has replaced Anna, and, once again, outwitted everybody.

Conclusion

First, who leads, guides, and influences whom? I think that both Carrie and Saul lead, influence and guide each other, much like family members in an almost symbiotic relationship. They are the perfect team to plan and execute CIA operations.

Saul is responsible for CIA operations such as bringing about by means of blackmail Javadi and Brody's elimination of Akbari, while Carrie is his best analyst with important contacts in the field. She speaks Arabic, Farsi, French and Russian. She also excels in her out-of-the-box thinking and courage in dangerous situations and sees what everybody else overlooks. Carrie always looks at the tiniest details and acts in line with her analysis of whatever situation she faces.

Although Saul is her boss, Carrie often acts independently, hence against his directives. She is the only one to suspect that al-Qaeda has turned Brody and begins a relationship with him to gather evidence of his betrayal. Back

---

[33] S8:E12.

then, everybody else in Washington, even Saul, is smitten with the American hero, but Carrie sees beyond his mask, which Abu Nazir has forced Brody to put on by means of psychological torture. While the team's SUV is being attacked by a mob of angry men in Beirut, she rushes up to Fatima's apartment to gather evidence and information. Everybody in their right mind would have left immediately, but Carrie takes that immense risk and finds material that incriminates Brody, thus providing the CIA with leverage over him.

Carrie needs Saul to watch over her when she doubts herself or suffers from depression, a symptom of her bipolar condition. Saul is her anchor because he accepts her the way she is and appreciates her commitment to CIA operations.

Carrie's loyalty to Saul has no limits: she lets herself be captured by the GRU to save the secret of Simone Martin's defection from the GRU to the CIA, paying the high price of her sanity. Her decision is completely rational: if her arrest by the GRU is what it takes to see through Martin's defection, that's what she does. She immediately understands that after Anna's suicide, Saul needs a new asset in Moscow. Therefore, she defects to Moscow, destroys for good her reputation as a CIA operative and makes Yevgeni believe that he has recruited her. Her book revealing past CIA operations is just a smokescreen for her cover as Saul's new Moscow asset, keeping GRU analysts busy with the analysis of the past, while she is providing Saul top secret information from the GRU headquarters now. At that moment, when she decides to defect, she knows that she can never go back home, never see her sister Maggie or her daughter Frannie, that her life will most probably end in Moscow—but she does it anyway. I think she planned her defection seconds after Yevgeni told her about Anna's suicide in Gush Etzion, when she was watching the cute little Israeli boys playing football. That's how quickly she thinks things through.

Who is more of a Machiavellian? I think it is Saul. He reactivates Carrie, whenever he needs her expertise and contacts, completely ignoring her fragile mental health. Saul uses Carrie for his plans because he knows that she will deliver results. Carrie is sometimes ruthless, when she needs to get information, but in a wider perspective the only dictum she follows is the first Machiavellian principle: be kind and provide stability. She always tries to save lives and achieve her operative goals at the same time. She breaks Brody in minutes, using their feelings for one another to make him confess. In that interrogation, she tells him the truth—and Brody senses it. That is why he confesses. He trusts her. Whom do I trust? I trust the person who tells me the truth, even if the truth does not shed a positive light on my decisions and actions. I trust the person who knows me and still loves me.

She tells Simone Martin about Yevgeni's fake feelings for her and lies to Dorit to get Saul's USB stick. Carrie also displays a deep concern for human life in situations she can gain nothing from, thus defying Machiavellian logic for the sake of saving a human life: at great risk for the teams, she saves Samira in Kabul and Fatima in Beirut. A 21st-century Machiavelli would probably have advised her to act the same way in both cases: forget Samira and Fatima, they have done their deed, they are no longer of use to us. On the contrary: trying to save them will limit our operational range now.

The prospect of nuclear war forces Carrie to threaten Saul, but she doesn't kill him, since she has a way out. She gets Yevgeni the evidence that Anna is Saul's asset. Too bad for the GRU that Saul was quicker, anticipating the GRU's arrest of his asset.

Saul shows his Machiavellianism when Carrie pressures him to reveal the identity of his Russian asset. He is not bothered if the US enter a nuclear war with Pakistan, since to his way of thinking, such a war is a regional one that the US is certain to win anyway. His asset is more important since Anna delivers information from the US's principal enemy, Russia. Considering the political context, Saul is correct, and as a cold-war warrior he has the big picture in mind. Carrie also sees the big picture, but always finds a way out.

Saul could never have pulled off the Javadi operation without Carrie's loyalty and her willingness to portray herself as a traitor to the CIA, upon which Javadi contacted her. At the high cost to her personal reputation, Carrie thus prepared the grounds for Saul's Iranian operation.

Second, is Carrie a convincing example of political sustainability and political efficiency? Yes, to both. Carrie is politically sustainable because of her loyalty and intelligence, her willingness to protect her country at her own personal cost. She is a stable factor for the CIA, always spot on, reliable, and endlessly loyal. Is Carrie politically efficient? Yes. How much more politically efficient do you have to be to have yourself, knowing what awaits you, arrested by the GRU?

Lastly, with regard to the three Machiavellian principles mentioned in the introduction: who fares worst and best in

Machiavellian terms? The three principles are: 1, prudence and humanity—or embodying kindness and stability; 2, the necessity of appearing to have good qualities—or good PR; and 3, the avoidance of being hated—or know thy subjects.

US President Elizabeth Keane deserves an Olympic gold medal for being the worst Machiavellian in HL: driven by her ego, she disregards all three principles. So eager is Keane to convince the US citizens of her capabilities as the first female US president that she is neither prudent nor kind, and that is the reason why US citizens do not trust her. Her PR, which she controls, against the advice of her loyal chief of staff Wellington, is so lousy that it portrays her in a negative fashion. The more she shows muscle, the more the citizens hate her; this is evidence that she is completely unaware of how her citizens think. Guided by her paranoia, Keane has lost the ability to understand the citizens' concerns. She is full of herself, shuts down justified criticism and does not understand that in politics, one's image is as important as one's unpopular decisions. Yet, eventually, she does step down, probably because she has begun to understand how wrong she has been during her presidency.

The Olympic gold medal for being the best Machiavellian goes to Yevgeni Gromov and Colonel Mirov, thus to the GRU, fulfilling Machiavellian principles I, II and III. Why? To the Russian citizens, deprived from a free press, the GRU's press conference at the UN in New York is a smashing success, since it portrays Russia as a prudent and kind global actor. The Russian Federation is factually right, and the GRU's analysis of the black box proves that the US is a war monger; the Russian PR is very convincing, making their citizens proud of the GRU and the Russian government, thereby avoiding citizens' hatred. To the mindset of a Russian patriot, the GRU represents an achievement of all three Machiavellian principles: kindness and humanity, good PR and know thy citizens. Colonel Mirov and Yevgeni are the embodiment of loyalty to the Russian Federation's political strength.

Again, in Machiavellian thinking, the political regime plays no role; democracy, human rights and a free press are not principal values to the Russian government, which concentrates on keeping its strength on a global scale.

A last word: who and what is Carrie? In the context of our Judaeo-Christian culture and Western pop culture, Carrie Mathison is the female saviour of the world. Carrie is Superwoman. Blond, attractive, and young, she is a Christian female icon such as Diana, Princess of Wales, emotionally shattered, psychologically unstable but pursuing the good for mankind while being authentic. The series HL is a product of Western civilization, and CIA agent Carrie Mathison is saving mankind, while promoting the Christian commandments of love. Carrie is not Jesus, but his messenger.

VI. Thomas Hobbes in New Mexico: *Breaking Bad*

Dedicated to Vince Gilligan: Yo, chapeau, man!

Introduction

This essay should be understood as an inquiry into the very successful US TV series *Breaking Bad* (BB).[1] I use political theory analysis and plot analysis as textual analysis of the story.[2] In the first chapter, I present a summary of the story of Walter White. In the second chapter, I analyse BB according to Thomas Hobbes' (1588–1679) *Leviathan*.[3] What Hobbes meant with his famous saying that man is man's wolf (*homo homini lupus*),[4] thus a deadly reciprocal threat of all against all comes to life in Walter becoming a full-fledged criminal, with murder and deception the tools of his new

---

[1] Basic information about *Breaking Bad* on https://www.imdb.com/title/tt0903747/; accessed 6 February 2021. The abbreviation I chose for *Breaking Bad* (BB) is, by my generation and in Europe, commonly understood as the initials of Brigitte Bardot (*1934), one of the great beauties of French cinema. In this paper, BB is the abbreviation for *Breaking Bad*. Cooking has never been a principal asset of Brigitte Bardot.

[2] As I am no trained professional in psychology, Todd Grande's YouTube channel taught me a lot. See Grande on the personality of Walter White: https://www.youtube.com/watch?v=8zrBZezqo_Y; accessed 10 February 2021.

[3] I quote from Thomas Hobbes, *Leviathan*, ed. by Richard Tuck, 2nd revised student edition (Cambridge: Cambridge University Press, 1996).

[4] Hobbes' 'war of all against all', on https://plato.stanford.edu/entries/hobbes-moral/; accessed 7 February 2021.

craft. Walter is breaking bad, [5] violating societal norms and ethical values, relentlessly pursuing his plans of making money for his family and enjoying his new role as a provider. The third chapter is dedicated to an analysis of how Hannah Arendt's definitions of power, strength, authority, violence and judgement[6] apply to the characters in BB. In the conclusion, I shall answer the following research questions: First, why is the global public still so smitten with Walter White? Second, what can one learn from BB for our contemporary *conditio humana* in the 21st century? Third, is Walter White the master of his life, thus self-determined (*Selbstbestimmung*), or is he dominated by forces outside of his own free will (*Fremdbestimmung*)?

I. Breaking Bad—Summary of the Plot

When I purchased my first iPad in the summer of 2015, I discovered Netflix and subscribed, overwhelmed by the wide offer of films, series and documentaries. I had never heard about the series *Breaking Bad*; anything to do with drugs was not my thing. On the web, a few months into Netflix, I spotted Sir Anthony Hopkins' (*1937) open letter to actor Bryan Cranston, who had played Walter White.[7] My first viewing of the five series took me about six months. Back in

---

[5] An explanation of the series' title by Vince Gilligan on https://screenrant.com/breaking-bad-show-title-meaning/ accessed 8 February 2021.

[6] Hannah Arendt, "On Violence", in *On Violence* (New York: Harvest: 1970), 3-87; "Personal Responsibility Under Dictatorship", in *Responsibility and Judgement* (New York: Schocken, 2003), 17-48.

[7] Sir Anthony Hopkins' open letter on https://www.vanityfair.com/hollywood/2013/10/anthony-hopkins-breaking-bad-fan-letter; accessed 6 February 2021.

2015, I was busy with a book project and did not have the energy and time to engage with the content. Yet BB had cast a spell on me, asking me to watch it again. So, I did in January 2021, prior to Switzerland's second lockdown.

My second viewing was a revelation. In the mornings, while skiing down the slopes, enjoying the snow, the cold air and the ice, my mind was in sunny Albuquerque. While scratching the snow off my skis, poles and boots, I was thinking of New Mexico's deserts, rattle snakes, tarantulas and the hilarious 1980s van. In the afternoons, I rewatched all 62 episodes. Let me now summarize the series' content. Naturally, I have to be brief here, since a detailed presentation involving all characters and the plot's sub lines would require a book in its own right.

The pilot S1:E1 introduces the main characters. It is the morning of Walter's 50th birthday; he has breakfast with his pregnant wife Skyler and teenage son Walter junior, who is 13 or 14 years old. Walter, further referred to as Walt, is a chemistry teacher at an Albuquerque high school and member of the school's Science Faculty. Skyler, who does not work, is trying to get published as an author of short stories; as we later learn, she has a professional past as an accountant. Walt jun., who later in the series insists on being called Flynn, an attempt to find his own identity, is handicapped with cerebral palsy.[8] Junior walks on crutches and his speech is somewhat slurred, but the illness does not affect his intellectual faculties, as he is a student at his

---

[8] See a description of the illness and its symptoms on https://www.cdc.gov/ncbddd/cp/facts.html; accessed 8 February 2021.

father's high school. The Whites' closest relatives are Skyler's younger sister Marie and her husband Hank Schrader, a DEA agent. Hank, humorous, loud and self-assured in his masculinity, is the opposite of the quiet, non-assertive, slightly depressed and polite Walt. When she is not working as a radiation assistant in a clinic, Marie indulges in shoplifting.

To make ends meet, Walt works at a car wash after school. On his 50th birthday, he does overtime at the car wash because his boss Bogdan is once more understaffed. While Walt is polishing a car, which belongs to one of his students, the rich kid immediately takes a picture, probably to put it on his social media site. Humiliation and the cruelty of others seem to follow Walt around. He comes home late, dead tired and has to be a good sport, because Skyler has arranged a surprise birthday party for him. The house is full of Hank's DEA colleagues and their wives, and Hank makes fun of Walt, whose intelligence he admires, but whom he does not really consider a man; he can barely hold the Glock Hank hands to him. They switch on the local news where Hank appears in uniform, informing the public about the liquidation of a meth[9] lab. Walt sees the weapons and bundles of dollars the DEA agents have confiscated and asks Hank about the money. More or less 700,000 dollars, is the answer. Hank, flattered that his intelligent brother-in-law is interested in his work, offers to take him on a DEA operation.

---

[9] Crystal meth on https://www.webmd.com/mental-health/addiction/crystal-meth-what-you-should_know#1; accessed 8 February 2021.

On the next day, Walt is rolling a barrel of washing solution at the car wash when he gets dizzy and falls down. After a check-up at the hospital, the physician tells him that he has inoperable lung cancer, and with chemotherapy a couple of years to live. He hides the cancer from Skyler and Walt jun.

As he promised, Hank takes Walt on a DEA operation together with his partner and friend Steven Gomez, known as Gomi; the three are waiting in their car outside a house because the DEA got a tip from a snitch that somebody is cooking crystal there. When the DEA agents storm the house, cook Emilio is arrested, but his associate manages to escape. Walt immediately recognizes him: it is his former student Jesse Pinkman. Jesse was such a lousy student that Walt had once graded his failed written exam with the words: "Ridiculous! Apply yourself!"[10] At night, Walt, who has looked up Jesse's address in the school's register, surprises him in front of his house, which belonged to his aunt who had died of cancer.

Walt blackmails Jesse into cooking, threatening to turn him in. Jesse has the contacts for distribution, and Walt can cook the purest crystal in town. They pair up, buy a recreational van, constructed in the 1980s, kit it out as a mobile lab and start cooking in the desert. Jesse offers local meth dealer Krazy-8 their product. Walt has no experience with physical brutality and is shocked when Krazy-8 and his

---

[10] S1:E4 "Cancer Man". Walt's "Apply yourself" has become an iconic quote of pop culture, translated into many languages: https://www.reddit.com/r/breakingbad/comments/zzwk8/jesses_old_chemistry_paper_graded_by_walt/; accessed 9 February 2021.

cousin Emilio, who is free again,[11] threaten to kill him and Jesse. He trades his and Jesse's life for teaching them how to cook the purest crystal; yet Walt does not cook crystal, he produces mustard gas which knocks out Emilio and Krazy-8. The sirens he can hear coming nearer convince him that it is over, that he will be arrested. But it is only the fire fighters who are approaching to douse the fire in the desert that Emilio's cigarette has ignited. The pilot ends with Walt crawling into the marital bed; his self-esteem and masculinity somewhat restored, he has passionate sex with Skyler who is surprised by his vigour.

In S1:E5 "Grey Matter", we learn that Skyler has asked Walt's former associates Elliott and Gretchen Schwartz for financial help. At their lavish party in their luxurious mansion, Elliot first offers Walt a job at Grey Matter; he should come back, since they need a creative and scientific new mind on board. Walt declines. He had invented not only the company's name Grey Matter but sold his shares for a $5000 down payment some 30 years ago. By now, the Grey Matter shares are worth billions. Gretchen and Elliot did not force him to sell his shares, but he nevertheless resents them and their wealth. His pride does not allow the Schwartzes to pay for his cancer treatment either and he is coming under pressure to hide the cooking from Skyler.

Albuquerque's crystal meth community is crazy about Walt's product: 99.1% pure crystal that comes in a clear blue

---

[11] Shady lawyer Saul Goodman aka Jimmy McGill got Emilio out; Saul is introduced in S2:E8 "Better call Saul". The series with this title is the prequel of BB, telling the story of Saul Goodman. At the time of writing, we are waiting for the final series 6.

colour.[12] Since Emilio and Krazy-8 have vanished, the former dissolved in Jesse's bathtub, the latter buried in the desert, Tuco Salamanca is now the main wholesaler-distributor. Establishing himself in the drug world to increase production, distribution and revenue, Walt puts Tuco in his place, taking revenge for Jesse's brutalization by Tuco's thugs when Jesse had insisted on being paid up-front. In a crucial scene of S1:E6 "Crazy Handful of Nothin'", we see a different Walt: his head is shaven and instead of his former teacher's attire in boring beige and a 1970s moustache he is now wearing black clothes, a black hat and sporting a hip goatee. Walt definitely looks dangerously up to date and milieu. Jesse's peers Skinny Pete and Badger probably would have complimented his new look with 'yo, awesome, man!'

In Tuco's office, Walt demands the money for the crystal Tuco stole from Jesse and an additional sum for Jesse's medical treatment. Tuco, who probably would score highly on Robert Hare's psychopathy checklist,[13] makes fun of Walt, assuming that what he has put on his table is a handful of crystal. He asks for his name, and Walt replies: "Heisenberg", knowing that none of the barely literate gangsters would possibly know who Heisenberg was.[14] Tuco's capacity for logical thinking is diametrically opposed to his physical brutality: why would Heisenberg come to ask for money and

---

[12] S1:E7 "A No Rough Stuff Deal".
[13] See https://www.researchgate.net/publication/318596156_Hare_Psychopathy_Checklist_PCL; accessed 9 February 2021.
[14] S1:E6 "Crazy Handful of Nothin'". A portrait of Nobel Prize winner Werner Heisenberg (1901–1976) can be found on https://www.nobelprize.org/prizes/physics/1932/heisenberg/biographical/; accessed 9 February 2021.

bring more crystal? Walt icily replies that that is not crystal, throws some shards on the floor at the window and bang, a huge explosion! Nobody dies, but the office is in a shambles. This convinces Tuco of Heisenberg's ruthlessness and determination, which demands respect in what is left of Tuco's crystallized brain. All the more so as stupid, paranoid and brutal Tuco can make lots of money with that Heisenberg. They conclude a business agreement up front.

Since they are afraid of Tuco's brutality, Walt and Jesse try to poison him, but Hector Salamanca, who is in a wheelchair and communicates with a little bell, warns his nephew. Tuco is about to shoot Walt and Jesse when Hank arrives. They hide in a ditch, and Hank shoots Tuco. The elimination of Krazy-8 and Emilio by the two cooks is only the beginning of what will become a killing rampage worthy of a very effective serial killer. I reckon, by the end of the last episode, Walt has killed at least 25 to 30 persons, with his own hand and by paying contract killers.[15]

A further gripping episode demonstrates Walt's intelligence and professional acumen: in S2:E9 "4 Days Out", they are cooking in the desert. The van's battery is empty because Jesse has made a mistake. For four days, they are stuck in the desert, the nights ice-cold and the days hot.

---

[15] Correlation is not the same as causality. Walt is not responsible for Jane's grief-stricken father's mistake that caused the plane crash with some hundreds of dead. Nobody forced Jane's father to go back to work while mourning. A somewhat superficial body count of the series' main characters can be found on https://breakingbad.fandom.com/wiki/List_of_killings_by_main_characters; accessed 9 February 2021.

Eventually, on Jesse's insistence, Walt constructs a new battery, which saves their lives.

The story of Walt and Jesse continues in a slow and painful moral descent, a Nietzschean abyss: "He who fights with monsters should be careful lest he thereby become a monster. And if thou gaze long into an abyss, the abyss will also gaze into thee."[16] Is Walt fighting the monster in himself? No, Walt does not see himself as a monster. He enjoys how his life is changing, the money he is making, because to his way of thinking, his motivation is ethical: he is providing for his family. Walt is first and foremost a scientist; if asked, he probably would justify his criminal activities with Darwin's survival of the fittest.[17] He is adapting to this abject part of society, the criminal underworld that is his money-making pool, because to adapt means to survive. The more crystal Walt cooks, the more money he makes, the more self-confident he becomes. The more self-assured he becomes, the easier he lies, making up convincing stories on the spot, without remorse. Falsehoods, after all, protect him and his family. The lies he tells Skyler, who feels that he is hiding something from her, seem to be like new clothes for Walt, in which he can hide and dress at the same time.

As for the second part of Nietzsche's apophthegm: the abyss is the criminal underworld, embodied by desperate

---

[16] Friedrich Nietzsche, *Beyond Good and Evil*, chapter IV, "Apophtegms and Interludes", no. 146, http://www.gutenberg.org/files/4363/4363-h/4363-h.htm; accessed 9 February 2021.

[17] Darwin's theory of evolution on https://www.darwinproject.ac.uk/letters/darwins-life-letters/darwin-letters1866-survival-fittest; accessed 10 February 2021.

junkies, sociopathic drug bosses, despicable white supremacy gangs and seemingly respected members of the community such as Gustavo Fring, the owner of the fast-food chain Pollos Hermanos. These characters are the abyss, and they are gazing back at Walt, eventually drawing him in.

When their team grows bigger, with Mike Ehrmantraut, who was Gustavo Fring's corporate security officer, now in charge of the business side, and Todd Alquist helping in the production line, Walt comes up with a brilliant idea: houses infected with vermin and insects need an extermination company to gas out the unwanted guests. Under the cover of the company, since the families have to leave their houses for a couple of weeks, Walt's team cooks in those houses, thereby moving production every few weeks to a different place, avoiding detection by the DEA.[18]

Walt has established himself fully in S5:E7: concluding a distribution deal with Declan and his gang, who control the meth market in Phoenix, Arizona, he asserts his strength and reputation, forcing his will on to Declan: "Say my name!"[19] Declan finally caves in to Walt's icy gaze, replying: "Heisenberg", admitting thus that not only has he heard of Heisenberg in Arizona, but that Heisenberg is the kingpin in Albuquerque's meth business, hence controls the New Mexico market. In the same episode, Walt kills Mike, tying up a loose end. Sitting on the banks of the Rio Grande, looking at the slowly flowing water, Mike is fatally wounded and so

---

[18] S5:E3 "Hazard Pay".
[19] S5:E7 "Say my Name".

fed up with Walt's ego that the only thing he has to say is: "Shut the f... up and let me die in peace."[20]

After Todd, his Uncle Jack and his gang of white supremacists have stolen Walt's money and shot Hank and Gomi in the desert, Walt has to flee. He goes to ground with the help of Ed, the disappearer, and spends a few months in a cabin in snowy New Hampshire, the Granite State. He is lonely. His desperate attempt to speak to Flynn on the telephone in a bar ends with his son shouting at him that he has killed Uncle Hank and he wants nothing to do with him. In the last episode S5:E16 "Felina", Walt returns to Albuquerque. It is his 52nd birthday, and he has breakfast at Denny's, arranging the bacon on his eggs sunny side up and hash browns the way Skyler used to do; he breaks the fried bacon into pieces and forms the number 52 on the plate. His cancer has returned, his hair has grown back, and he leaves the remainder of his money, some $9,720,000, with Gretchen and Elliot Schwartz. He presses them into taking care of the money for Flynn and baby daughter Holly. To make sure that they will arrange for a trust fund for his children and use only his money, he threatens them: at his signal, two red lights are directed on to Elliot and Gretchen's bodies from outside, and they naturally think the red lights are infrared from snipers' rifle scopes. Walt tells them that he has hired "the two best hitmen west of the Mississippi";[21] if they do not keep their promise, the hitmen will kill them

---

[20] S5:E7 "Say my Name".
[21] S5:E16 "Felina".

one day. In the car, Walt pays off Badger and Skinny Pete who have put some harmless red lights on the Schwartzes.

In their last five minutes together, Walt admits to Skyler, who has moved to a cheaper house with the children, what she had always suspected: his descent into criminality had nothing to do with his motivation to provide for the family. He enjoyed it and he was good at it; the criminal life made him feel alive. In a heart-breaking scene, Walt says good-bye to sleeping Holly, stroking her cheeks. From afar, he sees his son Flynn coming home from school for the last time.

At night, he takes revenge, killing Uncle Jack and his gang in their club house with an M-60 he has mounted on his car, activating the machine gun with his car key. Todd is the only one to survive. Jesse, whom the gang had abducted, kept in a dungeon and made a crystal-cooking slave, survives thanks to Walt who pulls him down to the floor; Jesse asphyxiates Todd with the chains of his handcuffs. Walt asks Jesse to shoot him, but Jesse refuses: he should do it himself. Jesse flees in a car.[22] The once infamous and brutal Heisenberg walks into the lab on Uncle Jack's premises, deadly wounded by a bullet of his M-60. The lab is professionally equipped. One can hear police sirens approaching. We see a slight smile on Walt's face when he touches the polished equipment. Police cars are arriving. He collapses, leaves his bloody handprint on one of the metal cylinders and dies in the lab, feeling at home and, perhaps, finally at peace.

---

[22] Jesse's escape to Alaska is the theme of *El Camino*, a BB film.

II. Aspects of Thomas Hobbes' *Leviathan* in BB

What is the connection of BB with Thomas Hobbes' *Leviathan*? Let me first present a brief summary of Hobbes' theory and then move on to interpret one major plotline, a keystone in Walt's criminal development: the elimination of Gustavo Fring.

Like all contract theories[23] after Hobbes, such as Samuel von Pufendorf's (1632–1694) *De officio hominis et civis juxta legem naturalem libri duo*, John Locke's (1632–1704) *Of Civil Government, Book Two*, Jean-Jacques Rousseau's (1712–1778) *Contrat Social* and John Rawls' (1921–2002) *Theory of Justice*, *Leviathan* is a thought experiment, inquiring about the rights of the sovereign, the rights of the citizens and why they should enter into a contract with the sovereign. The contract is the only ethical way of establishing political rule, since it is based first, on the empirical fact that political authority, not claims to be in possession of the truth, makes law; second, that citizens entering into a contract with the sovereign do this out of their own free will, thus on the basis of choice; and third, that it is rational to enter into a contract with the sovereign. For the majority of the citizens, it is reasonable and preferable to consent to political order than to continue living in anarchy.

Since he possesses political strength and the means of violence, i.e. the army, a dictator can force citizens to enter into a contract with him, but that would be a futile act, since such a contract would not be a real one, as the citizens would

---

[23] For contemporary approaches see https://plato.stanford.edu/entries/contractarianism-contemporary/; accessed 10 February 2021.

be bereft of choice. Also, the crucial element of rationality would be missing. Furthermore, a dictator does not need a false contract, as he already has the political strength, with which he governs, unbound by citizens' consent. A contract that is forced upon citizens is nothing more than pseudo-moral window-dressing of tyrannical or totalitarian rule.

Hobbes witnessed the English Civil War (1642–1651) and the cruelties and injustice it afflicted on the citizens; in his Paris exile, he wrote *Leviathan*. Naturally, the main theme of BB, Walt's descent into evil, has not much in common with *Leviathan*, save for an excellent illustration of two principal aspects: the element of anticipation and the state of nature.

Anticipation: Hobbes' realistic view of man is based on anthropological equality, which creates a situation of equal and reciprocal potential of threat. Men are equal in their faculties of body and mind; the weakest is strong enough to kill the strongest, either with a cunning plan or in cooperation with other weak men.[24] An example: how can a man who looks like Woody Allen kill a man who looks like Arnold Schwarzenegger? The weak one can poison the strong, kill him in his sleep or kill him in cooperation with others. From this anthropological equality springs the equality of hopes and goals, the situation when two men desire the same thing:

> "And from this diffidence of one another, there is no way for any man to secure himself, so reasonable, as *Anticipation*; that is, by force or wiles, to master the

---

[24] Hobbes, *Leviathan*, 86-87.

persons of all men he can, so long, till he see *no other power great enough to endanger him.*"²⁵

This equality of men and their potential threat to each other leads us to Hobbes' state of nature, the basis of his contract theory. The state of nature is anarchy, the absence of political order: no industry, no navigation, no building, no geography, no arts, no literature, no society. What rules is the permanent fear of each individual and the danger of a violent death for everybody.

> "And the life of man, solitary, poore, nasty, brutish, and short".²⁶

The state of nature is war of all against all, and because of the absence of law, power and order, man has to be wolf to others to defend his life, family and property:

> "To this *warre of every man against every man*, this is also consequent, that nothing can be Unjust. The notions of Right and Wrong, Justice and Injustice have there no place. Where there is *no common Power*, there is no Law; where *no Law, no Injustice.*"²⁷

Where there is no law, there are no rights. I can rob anybody anytime, and also kill anybody anytime without fearing punishment. Man's life is worth nothing without law, and only a sovereign can establish order. He who can gain political power is the future sovereign; if he is capable of

---

[25] Hobbes, *Leviathan*, 88, italics by me.
[26] Hobbes, *Leviathan*, 89.
[27] Hobbes, *Leviathan*, 90, italics by me.

convincing armed citizens to follow him and consent to his future role as sovereign, he can set the basis of negotiation with citizens for a social contract. If there is nobody capable of or willing to become the future sovereign, the state of war continues. From this follows that peace is a result of sovereign power.

Anarchy, war of all against all and anticipation as a means of survival is the state of Albuquerque's criminal underworld, which Walt joins of his own free will. In S2:E11 "Mandala", Gustavo Fring enters the story; apparently, as one later learns, he was born in Chile, moved to Mexico and from there to the USA. Gus' fast-food chain Pollos Hermanos is doing well, and Gus seems to be a decent and friendly citizen with perfect social manners who sponsors the DEA's annual charity run, sits on the boards of hospitals and can be seen every day in his restaurant, training employees and serving customers. Behind the law-abiding and generous citizen, however, hides a ruthless criminal who controls crystal and cocaine distribution in the south-west. Gus works for the Mexican cartel of Don Eladio who had sent Hector Salamanca and his nephew Tuco as the cartel's representatives to New Mexico.

Since Tuco's death, the crystal market is dry, and Walt and Jesse are cooking again in the van. Together with Skinny Pete, Badger and Combo, they are trying to build up a distribution network, but it is too slow and does not bring the revenue Walt was used to when they worked with Tuco. When a kid shoots Combo for selling crystal on the territory that Gus's thugs are controlling, their weak infrastructure is finished: Skinny Pete quits, because he is on probation, and Badger flees to California.

The ever-inventive criminal lawyer and lawyer for criminals Saul Goodman comes up with a plan: "I know a guy who knows a guy."[28] Through Mike, an ex-cop from Philadelphia, Saul arranges a meeting at the Pollos Hermanos restaurant, and Walt shows up on time. Jesse is late and high on crystal. That is why Gus does not make contact. Walt persists; he goes to the restaurant the next day and waits until closing time. Gus does not admit to anything but gives him a chance via one of his underlings. It is a test: place 38 pounds of crystal at a certain place, where $1.2 million is waiting for you. Since Jesse's girlfriend Jane got him on heroin and he is spaced out in bed, Walt has to break into Jesse's house, get the crystal from its hiding place under the kitchen sink, and rush to the meeting point to deposit it. He just makes it there in time and collects the money but misses the birth of his daughter Holly. Lying to his family is now second nature; the lies just seem to form themselves in his mouth.

Anticipation is the means of survival in Albuquerque's criminal underworld: if I identify you as a deadly threat to me, I have to kill you before you kill me. The theory is as simple as that, but the practice is much more complicated: time is of the essence, because I do not know when you are going to strike. First, I have to identify the threat; second, think quickly about how to deal with it while minimizing my own risk; and third, swiftly set my plan in motion. The

---

[28] S2:E11 "Mandala".

consequences of a mistakenly identified threat—that is, either I misjudge the potential of danger, or I identify the wrong person as a threat—are, in the worst case, my death, in the best case, the continuation of threats of all against all. I had better get it right and I need to do so in time if I want to stay alive and protect my family and property.

In S2:E12 "Phoenix", we see how Walt uses a situation to his advantage. It is not anticipation, but self-defence. What Walt does to save himself is not murder but failure to provide assistance. Jane is blackmailing Walt; she wants both Jesse's and his cut, otherwise she is going to spill the beans to the newspapers. Her plan is to go abroad with Jesse and the money. Walt goes to Jesse's house and finds the two in bed, again spaced out on heroin. Jane is unconscious and choking on her vomit, and Walt watches her die. Technically, he does not kill her, but he could have saved her by simply turning her on her stomach and getting rid of the vomit. But she is a threat to him, and her death eliminates the threat.

The most impressive acts of anticipation are Walt's elimination of Gale and Gus. This story is probably the most elaborate and complicated part of the plot, superbly written and excellently acted, like the entire series. To offer Walt, who has stopped cooking, an incentive, Gus has quirky-nerdy Gale Boetticher, a vegan chemist, kit out a professional laboratory. Gus hires Gale as assistant to Walt, because he does not do business with junkies; they are not reliable. But Walt wants Jesse as his partner, because Jesse just does what he tells him to do. I think that Walt really likes Jesse, like a son. Albeit Gale never gives him a reason to mistrust him, Walt conceives of Gale as a threat, because he is an academically trained chemist, hence a competitor. Even when he admiringly inspects the new lab, Walt is still rejecting Gus's offer for moral reasons. Yet, Gus, who can read people's weaknesses and strengths, knows which button to push: "A man provides".[29] He who stops providing is no man at all; if you are a man, you keep providing, regardless of your feelings or moral considerations. The offer of three months cooking for $3 million does the rest. Gus extends his offer to $15 million annually, contract open ended.[30] The lab is located under a laundry Gus owns; the people working there are illegal immigrants, hence used to seeing nothing, hearing nothing and saying nothing.

Walt's feeling of being threatened by Gus begins when the Mexican cartel, headed by Don Eladio, starts to put Gus under pressure in S3:E13 "Full Measure". Jesse wants to kill Gus's thugs who had ordered the kid to shoot Combo; Walt interrupts Jesse's plan and kills them for him by driving into them and shooting the one who has not yet died. Mike witnesses it and cleans up the mess, then he reports to Gus. Gale is back as Walt's assistant in the lab, since Jesse is in hiding and smoking crystal. A new thug called Victor is monitoring Walt and Gale's every move in the lab. When the Mexican cartel probes for Gus's weakness by stealing chemicals from one of his factories, Gus has to react.

Walt knows nothing about the cartel's threat to Gus. Victor monitoring them every second convinces him that Gus does not trust him; he suspects that once Gale has learned

---

[29] S3:E5 "Mas".
[30] S3:E9 "Kafkaesque".

how to cook his blue, he will be obsolete. He anticipates Gus's next move and asks Jesse, who is still in town, for Gale's address. If Gale is gone, Gus will need Walt and Jesse to cook. Walt is on his way to Gale's apartment to kill him, but is hindered by Victor, who is following him everywhere. Walt calls Jesse; Jesse shoots Gale because he is convinced of Mr White's logical arguments. Harmless Gale had given Walt a copy of Walt Whitman's poetry with a personal dedication to W.W. in his handwriting, which will later set Hank on to Walt.[31]

In S4:E1 "Box Cutter", we see Walt and Jesse being brought down to the subterranean lab. Everybody—Victor, Mike, Walt and Jesse—is convinced that Gus is going to kill the two cooks to punish them for disrespecting his wishes. From Gus's viewpoint, Jesse had made peace with the two thugs who had had the kid kill Combo.[32] By planning to kill them anyway, Jesse has broken his promise to Gus and the peace in Gus's organisation. Walt needs to be punished for helping Jesse kill the two thugs, and both have to die for killing innocent Gale, a valuable business asset in Gus's organization.

What happens then is a masterpiece of screenwriting: Gus, calm and collected as ever, comes down into the lab, takes off his clothes and dresses in lab gear. He does not say a word. This makes Walt so anxious that he is talking for his and Jesse's lives. His arguments are perfectly rational, appealing to Gus's sense of business: if Gus kills them now,

---

[31] S5:E9 "Blood Money".
[32] S3:E12 "Half Measures".

he will not only lose millions of dollars in revenue, but also end his monopoly on crystal production in New Mexico. Who can cook blue? Only he and Jesse. It will take Gus years to find new cooks as capable as them. The question is now, if Gus really wants to renounce on all the revenue, he and Jesse can make for him.

While Walt is talking for their lives, we see Gus going through cupboards and drawers in the lab, searching for something. He finds a box cutter and approaches them face on. He is standing at Victor's right, facing Walt, Jesse and Mike, who is guarding them from the rear. All of a sudden, Gus turns towards Victor and cuts his throat with the box cutter. Mike's face shows how shocked he is by this unexpected move. Gus's eyes are somewhat moist while he is holding Victor's head to the left, making sure that he is bleeding to death as quickly as possible. Why did Victor have to die?

Gus has changed his mind on the spot because of Walt's convincing arguments. Letting go of millions of dollars of revenue and shutting down an entire branch of his business just for punishment or the feeling of disrespect? No. Killing his cooks would also expose him to the cartel, weakening his basis for negotiation and eliminating his potential independence from the cartel. Gus is too rational to act impulsively, but somebody has to die, to put the balance right. In Gus's rational way of thinking, Victor deserves to die because he did not prevent the murder of Gale.

Walt and Jesse, who is off the crystal, are cooking for Gus, monitored by a different thug. Having seen that Gus is capable of killing a man with his own hands convinces Walt that Gus has just postponed their liquidation. He buys weapons from a black-market dealer.[33] In S4:E6 "Cornered", Skyler asks Walt to admit that he is in danger. Walt answers that nobody will come knocking at their door and threaten him. His reply has become iconic in pop culture: "I am the danger. I am the one who knocks!"[34] Walt suspects that Gus is driving a wedge between him and Jesse, when he learns that Mike and Jesse are running errands for Gus. He is also jealous, since he thinks that Jesse is becoming Gus's protégé. If Gus is turning Jesse against him, Walt has to anticipate Gus and Jesse's next moves.

Unbeknownst to Walt, Gus offers the Mexican cartel a one-time down-payment of $50 million for severing ties for good.[35] The cartel replies by sending a sniper, who shoots one of Gus's employees, a provocation that cannot be left unanswered. In S4:E8 "Hermanos", we learn about Gus's past with the cartel. A young Gus in his late twenties and his boyfriend and business partner Max Arciniega[36], a university-trained chemist, had made Don Eladio a proposal to cook crystal, a new venue for the cartel's business portfolio, hitherto focussed on cocaine. Don Eladio, probably just because it was Thursday afternoon, had Hector shoot Max

---

[33] S4:E2 "Thirty-Eight Snub".
[34] S4:E6 "Cornered".
[35] S4:E7 "Problem Dog".
[36] Gus does not have a family. He does not even order male hookers. After Max's death, Gus lives without love and friendship, completely focussed on his business as a basis for his revenge. Later in S5:E1, "Live Free or Die", the DEA finds a list of Gus's secret bank accounts on the Cayman Islands hidden behind a picture of him and Max. This is psychological evidence that Max and Gus had been lovers.

and left Gus alive to take care of the cartel's business in the USA; Gus emigrated to New Mexico and opened his restaurant chain Pollos Hermanos as a smoke screen for the distribution of the cartel's drugs.

Revenge is a dish best served cold. Gus hatches a cunning plan: to get rid of the cartel's top bosses, he needs Jesse to teach the cartel's chemists how to cook blue. This generous offer will convince the cartel that his loyalty to Don Eladio is firm, that Gus knows his place. Walt interprets Jesse's trip to Mexico as a further alienation, misjudging the situation. In S4:E10 "Salud", Gus, Mike and Jesse fly to Mexico. Jesse instructs the cartel's chemists; after the cooking, everybody meets at the swimming pool in Don Eladio's villa. Gus has brought a special present, a bottle of very expensive liquor. All cartel bosses have a drink, and while Gus is in the bathroom, vomiting his poisoned drink, they die. The cartel wiped from the face of the earth, Mike, Gus and Jesse make it back to Albuquerque.

Walt still fears that Gus is going to kill him. Gus threatens him in the desert: either leave Jesse alone or he is going to kill Walt's family.[37] Walt desperately tries to get Jesse back by convincing him that Gus has had Andrea's little boy Brock poisoned with Rycin.[38] Walt tells Jesse that Gus did this to convince Jesse that Walt has poisoned the little boy, that Mr White is a monster. Poisoning little Brock with the harmless Lily of The Valley is Walt's move to make Jesse come back and

---

[37] S4:E11 "Crawl Space".
[38] S4:E12 "End Times".

go against Gus with him. It works. Jesse returns to him, Brock survives, and Walt builds a bomb.

In S4:E13 "Face Off", Walt finally kills Gus, removing the main threat to his life. I think that Thomas Hobbes would have complimented Walt on his plan, because it is a superb demonstration of effective anticipation and cooperation in a state of war. Walt must kill Gus before Gus kills him, and Hector wants Gus dead as revenge for killing the cartel's bosses and the entire Salamanca family, the sociopathic killer-cousins in the silk suits and ridiculous boots included. How can Walt get at Gus, and quickly? If I cannot get to you, I have to make you come to me.

Saul tells Walt about Hector, who lives in Casa Tranquila, a home for the elderly. Walt visits Hector, who communicates with his bell and an alphabetical chart; Hector then instructs his nurse to call the DEA. He wants to talk to Hank only. The meeting takes place at the DEA HQ in downtown Albuquerque, naturally monitored by one of Gus's thugs. Hector has nothing else to say to the DEA agents than a very vulgar expression that begins with s and ends with k, but the point is that Gus's thug has seen Hector being driven to the DEA building and back home to Casa Tranquila. Since Gus must stop Hector talking to the DEA to protect his business, he visits him and walks right into Walt's trap. Gus has a syringe prepared to poison Hector. The time of his revenge for Max's death has come. In his many visits to Hector, Gus has always insisted that Hector should look at him, acknowledging him as an equal. Hector looks at Gus and grins. Gus's reputation with the DEA is flawless, but even with the cartel gone, Hector is still a threat to him, because he knows too much. Gus's plan to kill Hector is thus also an act of anticipation and he dies through Walt's act of anticipation. Hector activates the bomb Walt has placed under his wheelchair with the little bell and—boom! When Gus steps out of Hector's room, we see that half of his face is off, much like the robot in *Terminator*.

II. Aspects of Hannah Arendt's Political Theory in BB

II. a Power, Strength, Authority and Violence

Hannah Arendt distinguishes between power, strength, authority and violence:

> "*Power* corresponds to the human ability not just to act but to act in concert. Power is never the property of an individual; it belongs to a group and remains in existence only so long as the group keeps together. When we say of somebody that he is 'in power' we actually refer to his being empowered by a certain number of people to act in their name." [39]

> "*Strength* unequivocally designates something in the singular, an individual entity; it is the property inherent in an object or person and belongs to its character, which may prove itself in relation to other things or persons, but is essentially independent of them. The

---

[39] Arendt, "On Violence", 44. Empowering somebody to act on my behalf is based on the principal element of rational choice: I rationally choose the person most suitable to represent me, that is, my interests as a citizen.

strength of even the strongest individual can always be overpowered by the many [...]"⁴⁰

"*Authority* [...] can be vested in persons [...] or it can be vested in offices, as, for instance, in the Roman senate (*auctoritas in senatu*) or in the hierarchical offices of the Church [...] Its hallmark is unquestioning recognition by those who are asked to obey; neither coercion nor persuasion is needed. [...] To remain in authority requires respect for the person or the office. The greatest enemy of authority, therefore, is contempt, and the surest way to undermine it is laughter."⁴¹

"*Violence*, finally [...] is distinguished by its instrumental character. Phenomenologically, it is close to strength, since the implements of violence, like all other tools, are designed and used for the purpose of multiplying natural strength [...]"⁴²

Arendt's precise definitions are based on her superb knowledge of antique Greek, Latin and modern political theory; let us apply them to BB. First, it is mistaken to say that the cartel is in power or powerful. The institutions of power are those governing the city of Albuquerque, the state of New Mexico and the USA, since citizens have empowered the representatives to act on their behalf by electing them. Neither Gus's organization nor the cartel, albeit they are large groups, hold power, because their members have not

---

[40] Arendt, "On Violence", 44.
[41] Arendt, "On Violence", 45.
[42] Arendt, "On Violence", 46.

been elected by criminals to rule the underworld. Gus and the cartel have established their strong positions simply with violence and money. The cartel does business by the means of brutally applied violence and a rigid chain of command. None of the bosses holds authority, because the obedience of their thugs is based on fear, not respect. Between themselves, the bosses get along with each other as long as the cooperation remains financially beneficial to all, but if one misbehaves, he is a threat to the others, and they to him. Their appreciation of each other has nothing to do with respect, they tolerate each other for the sake of business. Is it not interesting that in many movies the biggest criminals, mafia bosses and drug crooks always demand respect and refer to themselves with aristocratic titles such as Don Corleone and Don Eladio? I think that, deep down in their hearts and minds, they know that even equipped with lots of money and arsenals of weapons they are just criminal lowlife, unworthy of true respect.

Gus holds authority over his employees at Pollos Hermanos, who respect him as a hard-working boss, but not over the thugs in his drug business. Gus's strength is on a very high level; he commands hundreds of employees, be it at his seven Pollos Hermanos restaurants or in the shadier parts of his business. His strength allows him to enjoy a certain independence, and once he has poisoned the cartel's bosses, his strength and independence increase. But as strong as he is, he dies at the hands of the incapacitated Hector and Walt who cooperate to kill him.

Walt's strength is growing in S2:E10 "Over". We see the family and friends in the Whites' house at a party organized to celebrate Walt's successful chemotherapy. Hank cannot take the chatter of the ladies any longer and asks Walt for something stronger than beer. They sit beside the swimming pool and drink whisky. Walt allows Flynn to have a drink with them, which Flynn enjoys. What teenager would not? Walt is jealous of Hank, because Flynn is talking to his uncle. Walt gives his son another drink, then a third. Hank tells Walt to stop and takes the bottle away, while Flynn is sick in the pool. Walt is very angry, his authority over his son threatened by Hank. He tells Hank to bring the bottle back: "My son, my bottle, my house."[43] Walt's ego tolerates no opposition. His fierceness astonishes Hank, who gives the bottle back. As a father, Walt loses his authority over Flynn, when his son learns that he had Hank killed. Flynn does not believe that Walt had tried to stop Uncle Jack and the gang. At the end of the series, Flynn is full of contempt for his once beloved father, and Walt's authority as a parent is gone.

Walt's strength peaks with Gus's death. But he faces another threat from the nine criminals who are in prison. They are Mike's boys and can tell the APD and DEA about Gus's drug operations and Walt's cooking. In S5:E8 "Gliding over All", Walt hires Uncle Jack and his gang to kill the nine prisoners. The operation is complicated since Walt wants all nine guys, who are in three different prisons, dead within two minutes. Uncle Jack's connections and Walt's payment seal the fate of Mike's boys.

When is Walt at his weakest? I think it's in the pilot, when the rich kid takes a picture of him, while he is polishing his

---

[43] S2:E10 "Over".

car. In that moment, the kid undermines Walt's authority as his teacher by mocking him. Walt's weakness turns into growing strength when he observes Jesse flee the house. That is the moment when Walt decides to cook. Jesse never questions Walt's authority; he addresses him respectfully as Mr White until the end, even when he warns Hank and Gomi not to underestimate him, telling them that Mr White is the devil.

Hank is empowered by the people since he serves with the DEA; he is thus a powerful member of the community he defends against the criminals. He also has authority over his DEA team; he is respected and enjoys promotion to ASAC, Assistant Special Agent in Charge.[44] The DEA agents under his command never lose their respect for him. Marie loves and respects him.

In BB, violence comes in two forms: the DEA and APD use positive violence to uphold the law and protect the citizens from the criminal gangs. The cartel and Gus's organization use negative violence as punishment and to protect their business. Walt uses negative violence to protect his family and the revenue from his blue, but, if asked, he would insist that his violence is positive, ignoring the fact that it was his decisions that put the family in danger in the first place.

---

[44] https://breakingbad.fandom.com/wiki/Hank_Schrader; accessed 27 February 2021.

II. b Judgement

Arendt on judgement:

> "There are a number of reasons why the discussion of the right or the ability to judge touches on the most important moral issue. Two things are involved here: First, how can I tell right from wrong, if the majority or my whole environment has prejudged the issue? Who am I to judge? And second, to what extent, if at all, can we judge past events or occurrences at which we were not present? As to the latter, it seems glaringly obvious that no historiography and no courtroom procedure would be possible at all if we denied ourselves this capability. [...] The moment moral issues are raised, even in passing, he who raises them will be confronted with this frightful lack of self-confidence and hence of pride, and also with a kind of mock-modesty that in saying, Who am I to judge? actually means We're all alike, equally bad, and those who try, or pretend that they try, to remain halfway decent are either saints or hypocrites, and in either case should leave us alone."[45]

Arendt's explanation of judgement applies also to judgements that we make in the present; my judging a situation prompts me to decide how to act, to make a decision. Judgement is thus the basis of decision-making. I can judge only if I am capable of and willing to distinguish morally good from morally bad actions, not only the actions of others, but also my own. Let me now apply Arendt's explanation to some of BB's characters in three ways: first,

---

[45] Arendt, "Personal Responsibility Under Dictatorship", 19.

morally good judgement, second, mixed judgement, and third, morally bad judgement or misjudgement.

Good judgement: The only character in BB who consistently makes good judgements is Hank, because he cannot be corrupted. Hank always plays by the rules and sticks to the law. Knowing that he needs evidence to get at Walt with the power and authority of the law, he convinces Jesse to help him provoke Walt into telling him where he has hidden his money.[46] The money is the evidence Hank needs. Apart from his upright character and rational and ethical way of thinking and judging, Hank also has a good instinct, a gut feeling for how criminals behave. By comparing Gale's handwriting in his lab notes with the handwriting in the dedication to W.W., Hank understands that W.W. means Walter White and not the poet Walt Whitman; he then swiftly puts his plan into motion. It works; with a faked picture made by Hank, Jesse convinces Walt that he has found his barrels of money in the desert and is burning it.[47] Walt arrives to save his money, and Hank and Gomi arrest him. The last phone call Hank makes is to Marie to tell her that they have arrested Walt.

Mixed judgement: When Marie learns the truth about Walt being Heisenberg from Hank and about Skyler's refusal to support Hank in building the case with her confession, she makes a good judgement of the situation at the White's house: she wants to take the children to her home,

---

[46] S5:E10 "Buried".
[47] S5:E13 "To 'hajlee".

protecting them from a criminal environment.[48] Skyler and Walt are criminals; Walt cooks blue, and Skyler launders his money. Yet, Marie's good judgement goes against the law; Hank knows that and convinces her that she has to leave the children with the parents. Otherwise, Marie makes bad judgements when she is shoplifting and showing up at houses on the market, pretending to be interested in buying. She knows that stealing is a criminal offence but enjoys the thrill that comes with it, much like Walt, whose cooking makes him feel alive. I think Marie visits houses on the market because of a psychological need; she is in dire need of attention. Skyler makes one good judgement: when she asks Elliott and Gretchen Schwartz to help finance Walt's cancer therapy, she does not know yet about his cooking. Yet, once she knows the truth, she not only plays along, overwhelmed by the money Walt makes, but comes up with a plan how to launder it: she convinces Bogdan with a little scheme to sell her the car wash. Marie and Skyler are morally flawed, the former by her shoplifting issues, the latter by her collaboration in laundering Walt's money.

Bad judgement or misjudgement: Lydia is a criminal mastermind in her own right and consistent in her bad moral judgement. She not only wants Mike's nine guys killed before Walt sets his mind to it but sets up Declan's gang to be killed by Uncle Jack and his gang in S5:E10 "Buried". Lydia is so ice-cold that she impresses even Todd, who fancies her. She dies a well-deserved slow death at Walt's hands. In S5:E16 "Felina", Walt meets her and Todd in the coffee shop and

---

[48] S5:E10 "Buried".

begs them to consider taking up business with him again. What for? Revenge. Lydia and Todd decline Walt's offer and do not notice that Walt has laced Lydia's sugar substitute with Rycin. When she, visibly ill, calls Todd, he cannot pick up the phone, because Jesse has just strangled him. Walt picks up Todd's phone and tells her that she is going to die from Rycin poisoning.

Walt's ego makes him misjudge Todd. Seemingly harmless young Todd is as ice-cold as Lydia. He is always very polite and seems to admire Walt, playing to his vanity and manipulating him into hiring Uncle Jack and his gang. It is a crude mistake by Walt, Mike and Jesse not to eliminate Todd after he has shot the kid on the bike in the desert. Todd's murder of the boy on the bike haunts Jesse, who has a soft spot for kids.

Finally, what are the two worst misjudgements in BB? First, it is Walt's refusal of Elliot's offer to come back to Grey Matter.[49] This is a misjudgement of epic proportions. Had Walt taken up that offer, he could have made a lot of money, bought back some Grey Matter shares, provided for his family, enjoyed the freedom of research and possibly won the Nobel Prize for Chemistry. But his ego makes him decline Elliot's well-meant offer. Elliot's offer is not charity, but a business proposal born from friendship and respect, yet Walt does not see it that way. Second, the DVD Walt and Skyler make in S5:E11 "Confession" is a major misjudgement, because Walt thinks that the DVD will stop Hank from going after him. The very idea of turning the truth around is

---

[49] S1:E5 "Grey Matter".

brilliant: we see Walt looking into the camera and saying that when you watch this DVD, I am probably dead. Then he tells his story: his brother-in-law Hank Schrader is Heisenberg, the drug kingpin in Albuquerque, who is hiding in plain sight in his function as DEA officer. Hank has been cooperating with Gustavo Fring who has threatened Walt's family. Hank has killed Fring and is now blackmailing Walt to keep cooking crystal. In the DVD, Walt presents himself as the victim of Hank. But why does he think that this DVD could possibly stop Hank from going after him? Walt, who really should know Hank, misjudges his brother-in-law's perseverance. He should have known that Hank will find a way to arrest him on the basis of evidence.

Conclusion

Let me now answer my research questions: First, why is the global public still so smitten with Walter White? Second, what can one learn from BB for our contemporary *conditio humana* in the 21st century? Third, is Walter White the master of his life, thus self-determined (*Selbstbestimmung*), or is he dominated by forces outside of his own free will (*Fremdbestimmung*)?

First: there are dramas that are so compelling that one cannot forget them, not because they tell a new story, but because they tell an old story in a new way. BB is a new interpretation of the biblical character change from Saulus to Paulus, turned on its head. Walt turns from Paulus to Saulus. He appeals to us because he is human. A decent man turns into a bad man, and we witness his descent into evil. We can understand why he is breaking bad: acting decently and always doing the right thing got him nowhere, on the contrary. Fate has dealt Walt a very bad card, and when he is diagnosed with terminal lung cancer, he decides to cook crystal: the money he earns will provide his wife and children with financial security.

Second: we can learn from Walt what not to do. If you choose the wrong path, you will have to deal with the consequences of your choices. This statement does not make our *conditio humana* in the 21st century any easier, but it promotes a clear message: you alone are responsible for your deeds, nobody else. If you think it is a good idea to cook crystal, you will end up like Walt: alone and lonely, hated by your family. If you decide to start smoking crystal, you will end up like the Albuquerque junkies, prostituting yourself for the next smoke. And if you think you have it in you to take it up with a drug cartel, there is always another person endowed with more criminal energy and equipped with better weapons than you.

Third: is Walt an independent actor, does he make his decisions of his own free will? Yes, absolutely. Nobody forced Walt to start cooking crystal. At the beginning of his criminal career, Walt's intentions seem to be moral; he wants to provide for his family. Knowing that he has only two years left to live, Walt turns, in financial terms, from a decent loser into a criminal provider, alienating the very persons he apparently cares so much for.

Who is BB's epitome of evil? I think it is Uncle Jack and his idiotic gang of white supremacists, his nephew Todd and greedy, ruthless Lydia, who drinks camomile tea, has a little daughter and no problem at all about having people killed.

Mike is the only one who sees right through her. Lydia's criminal energy knows no bounds, and she can always talk herself out of a threat, for example, when she suggests to Mike, Walt and Jesse to steal the methylamine they are short of from a train she dispatches every month. To Lydia, Todd, Uncle Jack and his gang, human life is just a factor, a figure and more often than not a simple nuisance. If somebody gets in their way, they just do away with them. So malignant are the activities of these characters that one would find it difficult to argue against the death penalty, were they on trial.

Who is the kindest and most altruistic character in BB? To me, there are two: Jesse and Hank.

Jesse is a young man, a graduate from high school, who has chosen the path of making easy money by cooking crystal. He also smokes it without a care in the world. He is only interested in having a good time. Jesse is not innocent; he has killed Gale and Todd, the former because Mr White told him to do it and the latter out of revenge for having held him in a dungeon. Jesse has a tender heart, especially for young women and children. Confronted with all the evil in the criminal underworld, Jesse is changing into a softer, kinder and morally better character; he is growing up. Jesse is turning from an immature little Saulus into a grown-up Paulus, hence the opposite of Mr White. He is very kind to the little boy, neglected by his junkie-parents who steal the ATM; he also pays for Andrea and Brock's move into a better neighbourhood. Jesse's main flaw is his feeling of being lonely, his need for company. He also displays a serious lack of thinking straight, although he is not stupid at all. Jesse has his moment of intellectual brilliance, when he suggests replacing the methylamine from the train with water so nobody would notice that the drug has been stolen.[50] Jesse deserves a second chance; in *El Camino*, he escapes to Alaska[51] with the help of Ed, the disappearer, after having

---

[50] S5:E5 "Dead Freight".

[51] Why does Jesse escape to Alaska? What does Alaska mean to the American mind, what place does it have in American culture? My friend Daniel E. Miller: "For most of us, Alaska is romanticized. It is cold, people hunt, there is commercial fishing, dog sleds deliver the mail, and there is plenty of oil. Those are the jobs we know exist, but we also know that Alaska is relatively poor. We also know that there is little in the north, with most of the cities in the center or along the southern coast." My friend Michelle Hale: "I live in Juneau, in the Southeast part of the state, [...] To me, living in Alaska requires a certain ability to put up with things. Juneau is an incredibly beautiful place, for example, with abundant hiking opportunities, fishing, camping, skiing; really great outdoor opportunities. But we have truly awful weather and in the winter it is often dark and wet for many months. Our latitude is 58 degrees. And you can't drive out of Juneau so it can be pretty isolating. A lot of people say it is "toughness" that is required and I suppose that is one way to put it. I rather think it is just the ability to put up with things. My family all live in Alaska and this is different than most Alaskans. In the 1970's and 1980's we experienced a population boom as the pipeline was built from the North Slope to Valdez, and most people in the state are from elsewhere. There is a strong streak of independence but a huge reliance upon federal funding, which a lot of people refuse to acknowledge. My family came in the 1910's on my mother's side, from Norway; and in the 1920's on my father's side. They were in fishing and farming and mining. Alaska means tolerating a lot of inconvenience in order to live in a beautiful place where wildness still exists. It was easier a few decades ago for people with criminal backgrounds to disappear in Alaska than it is now. Lots of people did that. With the internet, it is not so easy now. But I think that idea remains ... have you read *Into the Wild* by Jon Krakauer? And it is a strange situation, theoretically it is not for the weak and whiny, but there is huge entitlement here and that actually gets pretty whiny. For

killed the boss of the gang who made the chains that kept him in Uncle Jack's lab.

Hank is the American hero: faithful to his wife, disciplined, never giving up and suffering from post-traumatic stress disorder after having witnessed the turtle bombing in El Paso, Texas. After the shoot-out with the Salamanca killer-cousins, Hank recovers and undergoes months of physical therapy to be able to walk again. He takes a fancy to collecting minerals; Marie calls them rocks, and she is spot on, without knowing it. Collecting rocks is Hank's way of finding new ground, a solid basis for his future actions. Once Hank makes the connection that Walt is the infamous Heisenberg, he relentlessly pursues his brother-in-law. Hank dies in dignity and authority; he does not beg for his life: "I am ASAC Schrader, and you can go f... yourself!"[52] he says to Uncle Jack before he is shot.

Finally, is BB anti-feminist or anti-women? No, the series is just not about women. BB tells the story of a man's descent

---

example, the state pays a dividend to residents from earnings from past oil revenue. It has become such an entitlement that many people think their annual check is more important than pretty much any state services. Alaska has not been immune to the far-right extremes in the US, either. It's ugly and scary right now. Covid has made those extreme differences leap to the forefront. I was born in Juneau but lived in what we call "the bush" -- on a remote island -- when i was a teenager. That disabused me of a lot of the romance of living in the wild. Yes, people help each other, absolutely, in life-threatening situations, but they also get drunk and shoot each other. Alaska has an incredibly high rate of sexual abuse, alcoholism, and domestic violence. Probably Siberia does, too." Email conversation with Dan Miller and Michelle Hale from 16 to 25 March 2021.

[52] S5:E14 "Ozymandias".

into evil, how he changes from a decent Paulus into an evil Saulus. BB is art, fiction, and the story of polite but not truly kind Walt is one of the best dramas I have ever seen. BB questions our understanding of masculinity: what does it mean to be a man?

At a time when self-appointed apostles of social justice are shouting anybody down who do not share their cult's beliefs, Western civilization should remember what made it a civilization: science, tolerance, and law. BB is so successful because it is authentic and truthful, without preaching. BB simply shows us that the judgements and decisions we make, the paths we choose, will prompt consequences that affect not only us, but also those close to us.

VII. Voltaire's *Candide* or Optimism: *Better Call Saul*

Introduction

I know a guy who knows a guy! Saul Goodman—Speedy justice for everyone! These slogans have become instant classics in pop culture, introducing the character Saul Goodman to the character Walter White in the series *Breaking Bad* (BB). In this essay, I address two *personae* in film and literature who share a characteristic trait: Jimmy McGill, aka Saul Goodman, and Voltaire's *Candide*[1] are optimists. They believe in their good fortune even in hopeless situations, when normal persons would question themselves in a critical fashion, or then, become depressed or even suicidal.

Jimmy McGill's life is the story of a loser, a douchebag, who, against all odds, never gives up. As Saul Goodman, he enjoys some brief years of admiration, success, and wealth in Albuquerque, New Mexico; to evade justice, he goes to ground with the help of Ed, the disappearer. Saul Goodman, Heisenberg's lawyer, is literally, as Jesse Pinkman puts it, what criminals need on their day at court: a lawyer for criminals, that is, a criminal lawyer.

Like BB, the series *Better Call Saul* (BCS)[2] is superbly written and acted; subplots include the story of the middle-

---

[1] Voltaire, *Candide, or The Optimist* (London: Macmillan Collector's Library, 2006).
[2] https://www.imdb.com/title/tt3032476/; accessed 15 August 2023.

class Kettlemans who steal money from the New Mexico IRS, the state's tax office; the Sandpiper and Mesa Verde cases; the sad story of drug dealer Nacho Varga, and the fate of German engineer Werner Ziegler who builds with his boys the underground drug lab for Gustavo Fring. To present all these subplots would require writing a book on its own. Therefore, I shall limit myself to a description *cum* analysis, not divided into the contents of each series, but structurally organized according to the three themes I deem crucially important for the understanding of the *persona* Jimmy/Saul: first, Jimmy McGill's life until he calls himself Saul Goodman; second, Saul's relationships with the persons closest to him, and third, the end of Saul Goodman as a lawyer for criminals and criminal lawyer. In the conclusion, I compare Candide's fate to Saul's, focussing on what characteristic features they have in common. Note that I cannot present a detailed summary of Candide; I shall focus on those parts of the text that are the most interesting ones for our comparison of Candide with Saul.

I. Jimmy McGill—Who? Saul Goodman—Albuquerque's criminal lawyer

BCS begins with Jimmy's childhood, presented as flashbacks in colour, while the present, Saul's life after he has fled Albuquerque, is held in black and white.[3] Father McGill owns a modest grocery store in Cicero, Illinois, while the mother is

---

[3] I am no expert in film studies, but this colour scheme is interesting: it paints Jimmy's past as Saul in bright colours, setting it thus off against Saul's bleak and depressing presence as a criminal in hiding, always afraid to be caught by the authorities.

a homemaker, who loves little Jimmy more than her elder son Chuck. Little Jimmy is a quiet child, observing people; he immediately understands that there are "sheep and wolves"[4] when a con artist visits the shop with a heart-breaking story to extort money from Jimmy's father. The sheep are good-natured and decent; they are the victims of the wolves who advance in life with crime, manipulation, and ruthless selfishness. It is the wolves who walk away with the cash, leaving the sheep behind, perennially poor due to their naïve belief in the goodness of man.

As a teenager, Jimmy pretends to have slipped on a patch of ice in a street in his community, successfully suing the local government and cashing in; this con prompts his nickname or, rather, *nom de guerre* Slippin' Jimmy.[5] Now, every rational criminal would know that you can pull off such scheme only once, especially in your community, where everybody knows you. Yet Jimmy, and this is why I think he displays psychopathic traits,[6] keeps repeating this scheme

---

[4] S2:E7 "Infallible".
[5] S1:E1, "Uno".
[6] Robert D. Hare. *Without Conscience. The Disturbing World of the Psychopaths Among Us* (New York, London: Guilford Press, 1993), 34. The Canadian psychologist Robert D. Hare developed the psychopathy checklists PCL-R and PCL:SV, diagnostic tools accessible only to professionals. His definition and description of psychopathy is based on decades of diligent and serious research with his team. The key symptoms of psychopathy are manifested in two categories: those that affect the emotional/personal sphere and those of social deviance. Emotional/personal: glib and superficial; egocentric and grandiose; lack of remorse or guilt; lack of empathy; deceitful and manipulative; shallow emotions. Social deviance: impulsive; poor behavioural control; need for excitement; lack of responsibility, early behavioural problems; adult antisocial behaviour. Psychopathy is a

until the authorities find out and punish him with a prison sentence. Jimmy, the teenager and young man, superbly portrayed by Bob Odenkirk, is a congenial inventor of fraudulent schemes, a true con artist. To con people, institutions and the government is his art and nature, his way of expressing himself to the world, his true self.

His brother Chuck, played by Michael McKean, is already a successful lawyer in Albuquerque, when he bails out Jimmy from prison, obeying their mother's wish. To Jimmy, committing fraud comes as natural as washing one's hands or eating breakfast; it is a sign of success in his personal order of values. He has no remorse about his activities, but he does have empathy, especially for persons close to him, or persons he can use at a later point in time. Often, he cannot control his temper, but he never brutalizes persons. Given his criminal energy, he shows a rather touching respect for human life. When his temper flares up in microseconds, we see him screaming for minutes, destroying phone boots, chairs, or telephones, but he never lies hands on a human being. Although Jimmy lies, is evasive, and invents things on the spot, it seems that people cannot be angry with him. His mother adores him, and he has a way with the ladies: he is attentive, respectful and sports the cuteness of a harmless boy.

---

spectrum, meaning that one can score higher or lower on Hare's psychopathy list. I find one characteristic trait most helpful: psychopaths do not seem to learn from their mistakes, which is one of the reasons why they are criminal re-offenders, spending years in prison. Jimmy's ice-slipping scheme is such a mistake he does not learn from.

Jimmy has, furthermore, an acute sense of survival; he knows his place and can read dangerous situations lightning fast. Add to this his rhetoric talent and you have a lawyer knowledgeable about the grey zones of the law, the room between what the law commands and what it does not cover. Talking fast and convincingly to brutal Tuco Salamanca, who is intent to skin alive (!) the fraudulent skateboard twins,[7] Jimmy not only saves the twins' lives, but endears himself to Tuco. Needless to say that Jimmy's rhetorical talent peaks when at court. He is a psychological master manipulator, but he is also serious about defending his clients. We often see him at the men's washroom rehearsing his speech minutes before a court hearing. He is not lazy. Jimmy sings for his supper, albeit more often than not with a crooked voice.

Chuck employs Jimmy at the post office of his law firm HHM, Hamlin, Hamlin & McGill after his release from prison.[8] This menial job in the basement prompts two events that determine Jimmy's future: he meets attractive, ambitious, and kind Kim Wexler, portrayed by Rhea Seehorn. Kim, not talking much, has always time to listen to Jimmy's complaints; she is a young law student who, owing to her hard work, earns an HHM scholarship that sees her through her studies. Also, Jimmy meets Howard Hamlin, Chuck's partner at HHM, whose sharp mind, perfect social manners

---

[7] S1: E2 "Mijo". Tuco, consuming too much of the crystal meth he sells, does not make empty threats. Jimmy understands this immediately and appeals to Tuco's sense of fairness and justice, manipulating the rogue with a mental picture of what Tuco thinks he is: tough, but fair; feared and respected, but just. The twins survive, each one with a broken leg.

[8] S1:E8 "Rico".

and good looks immediately provoke Jimmy's hatred, born from envy. Howard's father and Chuck were friends, and Howard is like a younger brother to Chuck. Patrick Fabian portrays the rational, friendly but emotionally flawed lawyer to perfection.

Kim and Jimmy are friends, often sharing a cigarette outside, and inspired by her professional ambition, he decides to study law. Unbeknownst to Chuck, Jimmy enrols at an online study course at the University of American Samoa and, after two failed attempts, he finally graduates with a law degree.[9] As a defence lawyer, he frequents Albuquerque's court of justice to get cases, wearing a light beige suit and a white shirt, dressed like the unconventional TV series star lawyer Matlock.[10] He is resourceful and always on the prowl to acquire clients; he organizes bingo afternoons at retirement homes, presenting himself to the elderly with the catchy slogan "Need a will—call McGill!"[11] He meets Mike Ehrmantraut, an ex-cop from Philadelphia, who introduces him to members of the Salamanca clan who will draw him into what will become the story of Gustavo Fring and his plan of revenge to destroy Don Eladio's cartel in BB.

Jimmy's finances are miserable; all he can afford to rent is the tiny storage room at the back of a Vietnamese nail salon. To get to his office, he has to walk through the salon, passing by all the ladies who are having their pedicure and

---

[9] S1:E8 "Rico".
[10] S1:E5, "Alpine Shepherd Boy", Matlock on https://www.imdb.com/title/tt0090481/; accessed 16 August 2023.
[11] S1:E5, "Alpine Shepherd Boy".

manicure done. "Chokoloh, ladies, chokoloh" is his greeting when he goes to the office, which is also his home; if he doesn't sleep over at his brother's or at a lady friend's, he unfolds a sofa bed. Jimmy is not abjectly poor, as he has a roof over his head, but he is in constant need of funds. The scrappy yellow Japanese car he drives has seen better times.

But Jimmy does not give up his dream of being a successful lawyer. After Howard Hamlin has sued him for copying HHM brand exclusive attire and colours, presenting himself on a bill board as a member of the prestigious law firm, Jimmy organizes a scheme that makes him known all over Albuquerque: he instructs and pays a bill board worker to feign falling off the scaffolding and rushes up to save him.[12] A team of film students he hires for his various shenanigans, records the courageous lawyer, and the city's newspapers are falling over in their praise of him. This trick gets him some new clients, but he seems to attract only delusional persons, such as the oil millionaire who wants to create his own state by seceding his mansion and land from the USA, paying up front with his own currency, or the engineer who has invented a new WC that teaches children how to successfully poop.

Following suit to HHM's legal action against Jimmy and his other various shady dealings that have come to light, the Albuquerque court suspends his lawyer's license for twelve months in a disbarment hearing. Jimmy answers a call of a potential client, saying that he is "on a year sabbatical from

---

[12] S1:E4 "Hero".

the law".[13] In another scene, he tells a client who is wondering about the Vietnamese nail salon: "I'm letting a nail salon using my lobby."[14] These quotes demonstrate how aptly he always puts himself in a good light, twisting reality, facts. Jimmy is not only a con artist, but also excels as a spin doctor, spinning the truth around—which makes him a phantastic defence lawyer for criminals.

Suspended as a lawyer, Jimmy finds employment as sales assistant at a mobile phone company, and immediately sees the job's potential: he sells cheap mobile phones to Albuquerque's' criminal underworld. Then, he engages his film student crew to make advertising videos catering to small businesses, and invents a new name, drawing on his video company's advertising slogan 'S all Good, man".[15]

Saul Goodman is born at a low moment of Jimmy's law career. Once reinstated by the Albuquerque bar association, Jimmy registers as Saul Goodman.[16] By changing his name from James McGill to Saul Goodman, Jimmy does not re-invent himself; he just takes on a Jewish name in the hope to attract wealthy clients, severing ties to HHM for good. His hopes that Chuck would employ him at HHM after he got his online law degree were disappointed. Saul is struggling in professional terms, but he is not alone or lonely. In fact, he is quite a likeable person. Let us now look at the *personae* closest to him.

---

[13] S3:E6 "Off Brand".
[14] S6:E4 "Hit and Run".
[15] S3:E6 "Off Brand".
[16] S4:E10 "Winner".

II. Chuck, Kim, Mike, and Howard

Saul has four persons close to him: his older brother Chuck; girlfriend and later wife Kim Wexler, and ex-cop Mike Ehrmantraut, who introduces Saul to Walter White. Without Mike, Saul would not have become Heisenberg's lawyer, helping the chemistry genius to hiding the millions he is earning with his blue. Lastly, attractive, allegedly wealthy, and successful lawyer Howard Hamlin, Chuck's law firm partner and friend, is Saul's arch enemy.

Chuck is the typical American alpha male: he is honest, hard-working, sees himself through law school with stipends, has a superb track record in professional ethics and a great career as one of Albuquerque's finest lawyers. As one of the founders of HHM, Chuck is torn between his brotherly affection for Jimmy and contempt for his criminal shenanigans. Although Jimmy admires Chuck and aspires to become as successful a lawyer as his brother, Chuck never takes him seriously. Chuck simply does not believe that a leopard can change its spots. He sees through Jimmy since they have been children; he likes him, but he also tells him the truth: "You are not a real lawyer. The law is sacred. Slippin' Jimmy with a law degree is like a chimp with a machine gun".[17]

Jimmy takes care of Chuck, who, after his divorce, has developed an allergy to electromagnetic rays. Whenever Chuck pays the HHM premises a brief visit, everybody has to put their cell phones in a box, and laptops and room lights are switched off. Doctors do not recognize the allergy, and

---

[17] S1:E9 "Pimento".

Jimmy thinks that Chuck's condition is most probably a psycho-somatic illness, caused by his divorce. Jimmy's love and admiration for his brother is touching: he brings Chuck food, water, ice to store the food, the daily newspapers and is always there for him until that fatal moment when Chuck compares Jimmy to a chimp with a machine gun. When Chuck retires from HHM, he is psychologically burdened with having lost his prestigious lawyer's insurance that is proof of his professional ethics. Jimmy has pulled off a scheme at the insurance's office as an act of revenge. Chuck, ill and now bereft of his once stellar reputation, kills himself by pushing over a petroleum lamp that sets his house on fire. This act demonstrates to us how much Chuck loved being a lawyer, how he defined himself by the law. He dies of asphyxiation. Wealthy Chuck leaves Jimmy five thousand dollars, which is more an insult than a gift of appreciation. The only person who understands Jimmy's hurt is Kim.

Why does **Kim**, the attractive blond, intelligent, and talented lawyer get involved with shady Jimmy? She could do much better in terms of marriage and partnership. I think that Kim loves Jimmy for what he is: an underdog like her. Kim was brought up by a mother who was a consummate con artist, unreliable, a functional alcoholic who often neglected her daughter. Kim wants for herself what she never had as a child: more. She wants financial security, psychological security, a career, and a home. Her hard work earns her a career in law. But deep down, she still thinks and feels like the unhappy teenager she has been. Kim feels close to Jimmy, because she understands his struggle for recognition by Chuck and admires his criminal energy. Kim is an exceptionally talented lawyer but loves the petty criminal Jimmy. Why?

Kim is thrilled with excitement when she and Jimmy pose as trust fund siblings at a bar; naturally, this con is Jimmy's idea. They ask a loud, arrogant, and drunk banker for investment advice, and manipulate him into issuing them a cheque of five thousand dollars—on top of footing the bill for their expensive Tequilas.[18] The con operation makes her feel alive. To Kim, life with Jimmy is fun and full of energy. She always defends him, and they marry that the authorities cannot use them as witnesses against each other.[19] That seemingly rational act is born of love; they never declare their love, but their actions show that they have deep feelings for each other. Kim does not mention the L word, because she is too controlled and rational, while Jimmy does not mention the L word, since he cannot fathom what it means. With regard to feelings, Jimmy is all action, no words.

Although she receives a generous offer from the prestigious Schweikart law firm, Kim rejects it, opening a law firm together with Jimmy; but because of Jimmy's suspension, Wexler & McGill does not work, and Kim signs up with Schweikart's. Jimmy moves in with her, and the scene when they, quite tipsy, throw empty beer bottles down on to the parking lot at night, tells us a lot about Kim's psychology: she is thrilled with doing what normal people consider a violation of good manners or the law. Overstepping

---

[18] S2:E6 "Bali Hari".
[19] S5:E7 "JMM".

boundaries is what Kim is fascinated with, and Jimmy feeds this need of hers.

Yet, as much as Kim loves Jimmy, she is different: she knows what is right and wrong and can tell apart truth from lie. She knows that throwing empty beer bottles down on to the parking lot is wrong—and hastens in the morning to clean up. Jimmy, on the other hand, cannot be bothered, as he does not acknowledge boundaries. He probably thinks: last night, we threw some beer bottles down on to the parking lot—so what? Let the caretaker take care of this, it's his job, after all.

Neighbours' boundaries, good manners, and good behaviour are values alien to Jimmy's nature. In his mindset, the facts can always be twisted. Massaging facts, twisting reality and simple lying is what Jimmy is good at. In his view, right is what benefits him, and wrong is that which goes against his wishes. He does not have the moral capacity to think of values in abstract terms, let alone apply them to his daily life.

Kim finishes her career in law with the words "I am no longer an attorney", [20] after she and Saul have witnessed Lalo Salamanca shooting Howard Hamlin in the head at their home.[21] So shocked is Kim about the murder that she leaves him, telling him that they are bad for each other. But that is only half the truth—he is bad for her. She tries to redeem herself by leaving the two things she loves most: first, Jimmy, and second, being an attorney. By moving to Florida, dying

---

[20] S6:E9 "Fun and Games".
[21] S6:E7 "Plan and Execution".

her hair black and punishing herself with a menial job as an office assistant, she thinks she can escape Jimmy's psychological hold over her, to somehow make good, to redeem herself, to repent. But she is wrong—she cannot forget him; he is always at the back of her mind. In the evenings, Kim volunteers as assistant to a lawyer who works *pro bono* cases, defending clients who cannot afford a defence lawyer.

Saul brings to light Kim's fascination with criminal energy, while she makes him want to be a better man. She needs him for her dark side, while he needs her for his light side—and one might think that they are a match made in heaven, complementing each other, feeding each other's needs, much like a sadist and a masochist do.[22] Yet, the opposite is the case. Their relationship is, in fact, a perfect catch-22 situation, no way out unless they sever contact for good. Kim: 'I need you, Jimmy, to feed my thirst for overstepping boundaries, your criminal energy makes me feel alive.' Jimmy: 'I need you, Kim, to make me a better man, as I do not really know the difference between good and bad, it's all empty words to me.' There is no way out of this catch-22 situation since Kim needs that which Jimmy can provide only by ignoring his own wish of becoming a better man. If Kim is making him a better man, she can no longer feed from his criminal energy, thus must renounce on Jimmy's criminal energy that is making her feel alive.

---

[22] A silly joke of the 1970s that explains the relationship between a sadist and a masochist: The masochist to the sadist: 'Please, hit me, please beat me.' The sadist: 'No!'

We see Kim visiting Saul in prison in the last episode of BCS.[23] Why does she visit? Since he has gone to ground some six years ago, they have not been in touch, Saul hiding in Oklahoma as Cinnabon manager Gene Takovich, and Kim concealing her identity in Florida. By the time the Oklahoma police arrest Gene, Kim has submitted to the court in Albuquerque the details of her involvement with Saul Goodman, the details of Goodman's involvement with Heisenberg, and her witnessing the murder of Howard Hamlin. She has met Mike a few times and knows nothing about him and his work for Gustavo Fring, the founder and owner of the fast-food chain Pollos Hermanos. She does not know Lalo Salamanca, nor Saul's involvement with him. To her, Mike is just an acquaintance of Saul's.

Saul's career gets a remarkable boost thanks to **Mike** who introduces him to Heisenberg. He can now afford a Cadillac, designer clothes in all the colours of the rainbow, Viagra, and expensive hookers. His villa is equipped with Versace-gold-like kitsch that screams *nouveau riche*. The tacky furniture is what Saul likes; he does not want to impress anybody; he is just realizing his materialistic wet dreams. Saul does not have a problem with manipulating people, lying, and spinning the facts, but he does not wear a mask. He truly believes that his activities are the right thing to do, to the benefit of himself and his clients. In his crooked way, Saul is honest with his criminal clients and true to himself—that is why the local criminals trust him. They sense that he is one of them. As Heisenberg's lawyer, Saul is living the good life.

---

[23] S6: E13 "Saul Gone".

Jimmy meets Mike when he frequents Albuquerque's court to get clients and cases, at the beginning of his law career. Mike moved from Philadelphia to Albuquerque to be close to his daughter-in-law and his granddaughter. The chip on Mike's shoulder is the excruciating pain of having lost his only son Matti, who had been shot by two dirty cops. Matti was not corrupt; he was murdered because he wanted to expose the corruption racket in the Philadelphia police department. Mikes sits in the boot at the court's parking, overseeing the parking slots and collecting the fees. Often, Jimmy does not have either the cash or the confirmation slip he needs for free parking, and Mike sends him back every time. When they first meet, they immediately dislike each other; like Chuck, ex-cop Mike sees right through Jimmy, identifying him as a con artist, while Jimmy, full of himself and looking down on the old man, thinks that Mike is a loser, put into that job to make his life difficult: "Like a troll under a bridge, troll alert here!"[24] he screams at Mike. Yet, thanks to Mike, who also works as Gustavo Fring's corporate security officer, Jimmy can make a name for himself as a lawyer, albeit a criminal lawyer. Enter, now, lastly, Howard Hamlin.

Intelligent, attractive, blond and blue-eyed **Howard** was born with a silver spoon in his mouth: his father founded HHM with Chuck, and young Howard seems to be an alpha male too, but this is just his public appearance. The good

---

[24] S1:E2 "Mijo". Odenkirk's face and move impersonating a troll while screaming at Mike, who calmly sits in his booth, demonstrate his immense talent as an actor.

family, the good reputation, law studies at an excellent university and upon graduation immediately joining his father at his law firm—Howard is a member of Albuquerque's elite in financial, professional, and societal terms. Yet, he is emotionally shattered; always fulfilling his uber father's wishes, deep down, Howard craves to rebel, to choose a different life, to find himself.

We do not even know what Howard would have done had he had had the courage to rebel, to reject that wealthy lawyer's identity planned for him by his father. Would he have become a musician, a writer, or joined the Navy Seals? Or would he have become an engineer or an architect? Or would he have studied fashion design to become the Albuquerque Armani or the New Mexico McQueen, clothing the city's *haute volée*? Howard does not know himself; he is like a white sheet of paper, bereft of a sense of self, wearing the mask of a successful lawyer. That is the reason why he admires Jimmy, because Jimmy knows who he is. Howard is too weak to stand up to his father: he marries a woman of good social standing, works at HHM, is loyal to Chuck—and is in love with Jimmy.

I think that Jimmy's charm and criminal energy attract Howard as much as they attract Kim, but Howard never understands his weakness and fondness for Jimmy. After Chuck's death, Howard offers Saul a position at HHM, but Saul rejects that offer, because he hates Howard. Howard, on the other hand, does not understand why Jimmy hates him so much. One night, Saul sneaks into Howard's entry, and, in a foul mood, destroys his expensive car. Howard does not sue him. I think he is rather happy about the negative attention

Saul has paid him. If I am desperately in love, without the hope of my feelings ever to be reciprocated, any sign of attention of my beloved makes me rejoice—even if my beloved destroys my Mercedes. At least, my beloved does not ignore me. Howard is desperate for Jimmy's attention. Jimmy's hatred IS attention.

When heavily drunk Howard, after having seen through Saul and Kim's petty plot to destroy his reputation, visits them at their apartment, he tells them that he has finally understood who and what they are: "You won! You two are soulless! You are perfect for each other. You do it for the fun of it. You get off it like Leopold and Loeb, you two sociopaths!"[25] Drunk Howard tells them the truth: he is in debt, and his marriage is falling apart. What he does not mention is his motivation: Why would Howard be interested in the reasons why they are together? Why does he show up at their apartment? Why does he need to tell them that he has found out about their petty plot of assassinating his character? I think that Howard is desperate to gain a last sign of attention, his hopes for Saul's love shattered some time ago. But, as a last move, he wants to demonstrate to Saul that he is not stupid. If you don't love me—fine. But admit, at

---

[25] S6:E7 "Plan and Evacuation". Leopold and Loeb were two young murderers from Chicago, IL, who killed because of the thrill of it and to prove that they were too clever to be caught, inspired by their misunderstood reception of Nietzsche's Ubermensch. They proved wrong. See https://www.britannica.com/biography/Leopold-and-Loeb; accessed 29 August 2023. The superb film *Rope* (1957) by Alfred Hitchcock portrays the arrogance of the two young murderers, who are found out by their former house master Rupert Cardell, portrayed by Jimmy Stewart.

least, that I am as intelligent as you are, that I am your equal, that I know what you have planned to destroy me.

Howard's sad life, a life of obedience, of not daring to try to find himself, ends when Lalo shoots him in the head. Mike arranges the ultimate blow to Howard's reputation, setting a logical end to Saul's plot: he has Howard's car and body driven to a beach, places some cocaine in his car and makes his death look like the suicide of a desperate cocaine addict who walked into the sea. From my enemy's point of view, my death is perfect if my good reputation is dead, or, at least, in doubt. My social death is finite when my dear ones will have perennial doubts about who I really was. Character assassination is like distorting history: hitherto known facts turn into suspicions, and my good reputation was but a scam.

III. The End of Saul Goodman

We have seen Saul's character, and I have mentioned his lightning-fast thinking. Clearly, he is not stupid, but he is no Einstein either. Saul's capacity for anticipating danger and predicting his future comes to light in BB, when he is at his tacky office that displays a huge tapestry with the text of the US constitution, *We, the People*. Faux Greek pillars surround Saul's desk. Heisenberg is with him, and Saul has just called Ed, the disappearer. Knowing that the end is near, that the Albuquerque DEA, Hank and Gomi, are after them, he tells Walt: "If I am lucky, a month from now—best case scenario— I am managing a Cinnabon in Oklahoma!"[26]

---

[26] BB, S5: E15 "Granite State".

That is exactly what happens. In S1:E1, we see Saul, now sporting a moustache and working long hours as the manager of a Cinnabon café in an Oklahoma shopping mall. The new identity he got from Ed, the disappearer, is Gene Takovich. After work, Gene drinks at home and watches old videos that show his past as Saul Goodman; he clearly misses his old life. He has a flashback, remembering an episode of his past. Hiding with Walt in the cellar of Ed's house, they have only each other to talk to. They know that they soon will leave, each on his own, that they will never see each other again. These are Ed's rules. Arrogant Walt asks Saul what time he would choose if he had a time machine at his disposal, bringing up the theme of having regrets.[27] Walt says that he regrets only that he sold his shares of *Grey Matter* years ago for a sandwich. Saul replies: "I got one—when I was twenty-two, slippin, I hurt myself." Walt replies: "So you were always like this", putting the finger right on Jimmy's inability to critically look at his past actions and decisions. Walt has changed, from Paulus to Saulus, while Jimmy aka Saul never changes. Jimmy has no regrets about his criminal behaviour; he only regrets that he had hurt himself during his con.

In Oklahoma, Gene manages to feed his need for criminal activity one last time. He instructs Jeff, the nephew of Maryan, an old lady whom Gene befriends, to steal expensive clothing from a luxury shopping mall. He trains Jeff, and the plan works. Gene also invents an identity theft scheme: impersonating a harmless karaoke singer at a bar, he meets drunk and lonely customers whom he gets back home with a

---

[27] S6:E13 "Saul Gone".

taxi, feigning to be a helpful new friend. The next day, Jeff, the taxi driver, enters their homes with the copies of the house keys Gene has made and steals their social security numbers, credit card and bank account details.

Yet, Maryan, the elderly lady, does not trust over-friendly and charming Gene. She checks the web and finds the arrest warrant of Saul Goodman, calls the police—and the police finally arrest Gene aka Saul aka Jimmy. Had he laid low, kept working at Cinnabon, controlled his need for criminal activity and then, perhaps, moved to Alaska to open a lawyer's practice under a new identity, the police would have never found him. But Gene simply cannot live without the thrill of his cons. So strong is his need for committing crime that he becomes reckless—and is caught.

At the trial that takes place in Albuquerque, Saul defends himself in his usual manner, putting all the blame on Walter White aka Heisenberg, whom he thought had been a decent high school teacher who had inherited some money. Attorney Goodman was as much a victim of Heisenberg as everybody else. He can convince the jury, who sentences him to seven and a half years of prison for professional neglect.

Then, something crucial happens: Saul is asked to witness against Kim, who has accused herself of involvement with Heisenberg and Saul Goodman, and as a witness of the murder of Howard Hamlin. His testimony will lead to a court case against Kim. Jimmy changes his mind: for the first time in his life, he tells the truth to protect Kim. He admits to all the crimes he had committed to launder and hide Heisenberg's money, insisting to be called McGill. The jury convicts him to a sixty-eight-year prison sentence.

In the final scene of BCS, we see Kim leaving the prison, and, in my first viewing, I thought that their relationship is over, for good. Yet, I had a nagging feeling, something did not add up, something in their past behaviour. I watched the final scene again and again and changed my mind. I have come to the conclusion that Kim thinks that has been her last visit, lying to herself, but, I think, after a month or two, she will start to visit him in prison on a regular basis. The reason why they have not been in touch for six years, Kim hiding in Florida and Jimmy in Oklahoma, was love: they both knew that contacting each other would set the authorities on to them. Because they love each other, they want to see the other safe—and if silence, a no contact regime is what it takes, that's what they do. Such is the power of love—it is forgiving, and, at the end of the day, born of an inherent optimism that is close to a delusional state of mind, because it defeats reality. To Kim and Jimmy, love as a feeling and optimism as a mindset to face whatever life throws at them are therefore intrinsically connected, because they are the means of their survival in difficult times.

Conclusion

Voltaire's *Candide* is the story of a young man from Westphalia who lives in cruel times; in the 18th century, war, rape, abduction, torture, execution, and occupation by foreign troops form the fabric of daily life more often than peace, material prosperity and personal security. Yet, Candide learns from his mentor, Dr Pangloss, he who speaks many languages, a polyglot we would call him today, one principle that shall guide him through life: "Things cannot be otherwise than they are; for as all things have been created for some end, they must necessarily be created for the best end."[28]

This way of thinking, that everything is for the best, that every cruel situation has a positive aspect and shall find a positive end, is the principle of Candide's rather simplistic view of life. Even when two soldiers shanghai him into the Bulgarian army, Candide is convinced that that is to the best: yet, to whose best, the world's or his? When he hears that Miss Cunegund, his love, has been raped and killed in her Westphalian Castle, desperate Candide asks where the best of worlds is now, fainting upon hearing the details. Candide's life is a journey through the world and its various cultures and political systems, a world prior to the glorious French Revolution of 1789.

In Portugal, Pangloss is hanged, while Candide is condemned to public flagellation; the local inquisition has accused them of heresy. Whenever he faces atrocities, legal injustice, or rather, the absence of justice, Candide questions Pangloss' philosophical principle but he keeps believing in it because he has not found another principle that guides him through life, that keeps him alive: "If this is the best of all possible worlds, what are the others? If I had only been whipped, I could have put up with it, as I did among the Bulgarians, but, Oh my dear Pangloss! Thou greatest of philosophers! That ever I should live to see thee hanged, without knowing for what!"[29]

---

[28] Voltaire, *Candide*, 4.
[29] Voltaire, *Candide*, 22.

An old woman takes care of him, and once his wounds have healed, she brings him to Cunegund, who is alive—much to Candide's joy. The object of his love tells him about how she has survived, having been sold to various wealthy men, because she is of aristocratic descent, thus has some value. Cunegund, Candide, and the old woman survive the earthquake of 1755 that destroys Lissabon, and travel to Buenos Aires. The story of the old woman's life is even more brutal than what Cunegund had had to endure.[30]

Candide has to flee again as the inquisition is after him. He leaves Cunegund and the old woman behind and acquires a servant named Cacambo. With Cacambo, he travels to Paraguay, El Dorado, a legendary land of gold in the Americas, Peru, and Surinam in Asia. On their way into the town, they see a black slave who is sitting on the floor, waiting for his Dutch master. He has one leg and one arm. This encounter prompts Candide to doubt for the first time Pangloss' philosophical principle:

---

[30] I am by no means a Voltaire expert, but the champion of the Enlightenment describes the suffering of men and women in the cruellest details, women naturally being subject to sexual torture that is hard for us to read today. The suffering of the civilian population under occupation by a foreign army and under the terror regime of the Catholic inquisition reveal Voltaire's humanism and the sense of Candide he wanted his readers to understand: the suffering will continue as long as the aristocracy and clergy are in power. Therefore, I think, *Candide* is a revolutionary text, intellectually preparing the French Revolution of 1789. A superb biography is Roger Pearson, *Voltaire Almighty. A Life in the Pursuit of Freedom* (London: Bloomsbury, 2006).

"Yes, Sir', said the negro; 'it is the custom here. They give a pair of cotton drawers twice a year, and that is all our covering. When we labour in the sugarworks, and the mill happens to snatch hold of a finger, they instantly chop off our hand, and when we attempt to run away, they cut off a leg. Both these cases have happened to me, and it is at this expense that you eat sugar in Europe; [...] 'O Pangloss!' cried out Candide, [...] I find myself, after all, obliged to renounce thy Optimism,' 'Optimism!' said Cacambo, 'what is that?' 'Alas!' replied Candide, 'it is the obstinacy of maintaining that everything is best when it is worst.'[31]

Voltaire was such a talented satirist and writer that he managed to disguise a rebellious political statement that would have qualified as high treason with a happy end of a rather banal love story, revoking our Western civilisation's happy end, the Garden of Eden. Paradise Lost, Paradise Gained or No Paradise at all? I think that Voltaire would have answered that there is no paradise; paradise is a figment of illusion pushed forward by the powerful Catholic Church, driven by its aim to keep the masses uneducated, superstitious, anxious, and therefore, easy to manipulate.

Candide, Martin, an elderly scholar, and Dr Pangloss, liberated by Candide from slave labour on a galley, find refuge on a farm in the Ottoman Empire, after they have liberated Cunegund and the old woman from a Transylvanian castle.

---

[31] Voltaire, *Candide*, 73, 74.

Candide wants, after all they have been through, finally marry Cunegund, his love, but her brother, the baron, whom he had liberated from the galley together with Pangloss, refuses. Candide is not good enough to marry his sister, because he is not aristocracy. This is Voltaire's critique of aristocracy, or rather, the delusional arrogance of the Westphalian baron who would have died a miserable death on the galley had not Candide, a nobody like Jimmy McGill, liberated him.

Candide and his little family enjoy their little farm; it is their personal Garden of Eden, their paradise. Cunegund is no longer the beautiful maiden Candide fell in love with when he first saw her at her castle. She is ugly and old, but alive. Candide has saved them all. Their future is bright, since they are, for the first time in their lives, free, oppressed by no political regime, and safe, as the almighty Catholic inquisition has no power in the Ottoman Empire.

Let me conclude with two quotes that demonstrate Candide and Saul's motto of survival: Optimism.

> "'There is a concatenation of all events in the best of possible worlds; for, in short, had you not been kicked out of a fine castle by the backside for the love of Miss Cunegund, had you not been put into the Inquisition, had you not travelled over America on foot, had you not run the Baron through the body, and had you not lost all your sheep which you brought from the good country of El Dorado, you would not have been here to eat preserved citrons and pistachio-nuts.' 'Excellently

observed', answered Candide, 'but let us take care of our garden.'"[32]

The past is gone, and I cannot change it. Therefore, let us look to the future. When Kim visits Jimmy in prison, she is puzzled: "You had them down to seven years." Jimmy replies: "Sixty-eight years, but with good behaviour, who knows."[33]

---

[32] Voltaire, *Candide*, 134.
[33] S6:E13 "Saul Gone".

Appendix

Index

1968 25, 40, 108
A Zory Sdes' Tyxhyie (The Dawns here are Quiet) 39
Abu Ahmad 63, 64, 65, 66, 67, 68, 70, 71, 72, 75, 76, 77, 80, 109
Abu Nazir 157, 161, 162, 164, 166, 167, 168, 169, 170, 171, 173, 174, 191
affirmative action 26, 27
Alaska 208, 233, 256
aliya 58
al-Qaeda 161, 162, 164, 166, 190
American hero 162, 165, 191, 234
ancient Greeks 116
Andrei Kuznetsov 184, 185
Ann Atwater 29, 30
Anna Pomerantsova 185
Anne Heche 31
Anthony Hopkins 198
anthropological equality 210
anticipation 210, 212, 214, 220, 221
Apply yourself! 201
Arab Jew 78
Arafat 83
Aristotle 15, 116, 143
Arnold Schwarzenegger 210
art 18, 41, 235, 240

ASAC 225, 234
Aufklärung 46, 53
Augustine 17, 113, 114, 116, 117, 118, 119, 120, 135, 136, 137
authority 43, 44, 48, 154, 180, 198, 209, 221, 222, 223, 224, 225, 227, 234
Barack Obama 25
Beau Bridges 180
behaviour 21, 22, 23, 24, 25, 65, 76, 131, 134, 138, 139, 144, 149, 156, 239, 248, 255, 257, 262
bipolar 165, 191
black box 181, 182, 183, 187, 194
blue 72, 141, 144, 146, 202, 216, 217, 219, 225, 228, 245, 251
Bob Odenkirk 240, 251
Brigitte Bardot 197
Bryan Cranston 198
Camille Paglia 41
Candide ou l'Optimisme 14
Capitalism 46
Captain Ayub 64, 68, 74, 76, 93
Caracas 173
caritas 117, 118, 119, 120, 135, 136, 137, 142, 145

Carl Djerassi 41
causality 204
ceasefire 55, 56, 66, 86, 96, 106, 107, 108, 109, 111
Celtic fringe 21
Charlie Hebdo 105
charrette 33, 34, 35
chess 187, 188, 189
Chuck Norris 79
CIA 7, 18, 151, 152, 156, 161, 162, 163, 165, 168, 169, 170, 171, 172, 173, 174, 175, 176, 177, 178, 179, 183, 184, 186, 187, 189, 190, 191, 193, 195
Civil War 22, 165
civilization 57, 143, 144, 145, 146, 187, 195, 235
Claiborne Paul Ellis 29, 30, 31, 33, 34, 35, 36
Claire Danes 156
Code Civil Des Français 45
compromise 66, 72, 107, 113, 116
conditio humana 198, 230, 231
contract theories 209
Correlation 204
Costa Ronin 157
cruelty 130, 159, 200
cupiditas 117, 119, 136, 137, 145
Cyrano de Bergerac 37
Dakota Johnson 126
Damian Lewis 157
Danesh Akbari 173, 174, 175, 190

Dar Adal 169, 174
David Ben-Gurion 58
David Bowie 37
David Hume 145
DEA 200, 201, 206, 212, 218, 220, 224, 225, 230, 254
democratisation 56
direct democracy 145, 146
Don Eladio 212, 215, 218, 219, 223, 242
Doris Day 39
Doron Kavilio 63, 70, 78, 82
East Berlin 108, 184, 185
Ed Harris 124, 139
Ed, the disappearer 207, 233, 237, 254, 255
Edmund Husserl 117
education 21, 22, 23, 29, 36, 44, 45, 46, 47, 50, 51, 137, 145, 164
Eli Cohen 64, 175
Elizabeth Keane 157, 176, 177, 194
Elizabeth Marvel 157
English Civil War 210
Enlightenment 14, 36, 46, 53, 143, 259
euthanasia 31
F. Murray Abraham 169
FBI 171
Feminism 17, 41, 52
football 181, 186, 189, 192
fortuna 153, 154
French Revolution 45, 56, 120, 258, 259
Gabi 64, 66, 67, 73, 74, 75, 76, 77, 82, 83, 84, 85, 88,

89, 90, 91, 92, 93, 94, 95, 96, 98, 99, 100, 101, 103, 104, 109, 110
Gaza strip 59, 83
Golan Heights 97
Golda Meir 58
Graham Greene 177
Grey Matter 202, 229, 255
GRU 157, 176, 177, 178, 179, 180, 181, 183, 184, 185, 186, 187, 189, 190, 191, 193, 194
Gush Etzion 185, 192
Gustavo Fring 206, 209, 212, 230, 238, 242, 250, 251
Hamas 17, 64, 66, 68, 69, 70, 71, 72, 74, 75, 76, 77, 78, 79, 80, 82, 83, 84, 85, 89, 92, 93, 98, 104, 108, 111
Hannah Arendt 17, 18, 27, 41, 43, 110, 111, 113, 114, 115, 116, 117, 118, 119, 135, 137, 154, 184, 198, 221, 222, 226
Hebrew 59, 78, 79, 82, 95
Hebron 59, 93, 95
Hector Salamanca 204, 212
Hegel 13, 14, 15, 16
Heidelberg 16
Heisenberg 203, 206, 208, 227, 230, 234, 237, 245, 250, 254, 256
Hezbollah 17, 69, 84, 93, 94, 96, 98, 99, 103, 108, 167, 168
HHM 241, 243, 244, 245, 251, 252

High Noon 72
Hollywood 14
hour zero 87
Howard Hamlin 241, 243, 245, 248, 250, 251, 256
HQ 65, 66, 68, 69, 70, 76, 84, 86, 88, 93, 95, 96, 97, 98, 100, 101, 103, 109, 161, 162, 168, 169, 171, 220
hygiene 24, 32
I am the one who knocks! 218
I know a guy who knows a guy! 237
inquisition 258, 259, 261
Iran 69, 100, 108, 167, 172, 173, 175
Isabelle Adjani 42
Isis 69, 77, 79, 80, 83, 86, 91, 92
Israel 58, 64, 68, 69, 73, 77, 79, 83, 87, 88, 90, 94, 100, 103, 106, 108, 110, 111, 167, 186
Jan Patočka 117
Jane Birkin 38
Jenin 59, 94, 95, 96, 97, 98, 99, 102, 103, 104
Jews 30, 32, 45, 58, 68, 73, 109
Jimmy McGill 202, 237, 238, 241, 242, 244, 247, 256, 261
Jon Krakauer 233
Kant 7, 17, 46, 53, 55, 56, 59, 60, 61, 62, 63, 105, 106, 109

Kim Wexler 241, 245, 247
Königsberg 56
Ku Klux Klan 16
La Serenissima 56, 57
laicism 45
Leibniz 13, 14
Leopold and Loeb 253
Leviathan 143, 188, 197, 209, 210, 211
Lior Raz 63, 110
Locke 143, 209
Logos 15, 121
Lubyanka 186
Major General Majid Javadi 172, 173, 174, 175, 190, 193
Mandy Patinkin 156
Marco Polo 57
martial law 181
Martin Heidegger 117
Martin Luther King Jr. 25
Marx 46
Mary 31, 35, 41, 142
Mary Beard 41
Matlock 242
Max Horkheimer 14
Merab Ninidze 157
meth 200, 201, 202, 206, 241
Michael McKean 240
Mike Ehrmantraut 206, 242, 245
Mississippi 207
Molière 42, 47
Montaigne 143
Montesquieu 143
multiculturalism 44

NAACP 33
Nablus 66, 79, 80, 87, 88, 90
narcissism 113, 116, 144
nepotism 58
New Hampshire 207
Niccolò Machiavelli 7, 18, 151, 153, 154, 155, 159, 160, 161, 192
Nicholas Brody 156, 157, 161, 162, 163, 164, 165, 166, 167, 168, 169, 170, 171, 172, 173, 174, 175, 189, 190, 192
Nidal al-Makdasi 77, 80, 85, 91, 109
Nietzschean abyss 205
nouveau riche 250
nuclear war 146, 182, 183, 185, 188, 193
Olivia Colman 124
Pacifism 107
Palestinian authority 69
Palestinians 59, 69, 73, 76, 79, 90, 106, 110
Patrick Fabian 242
Peter Quinn 169, 170
Plutarch 17, 113, 114, 120, 121, 122, 135
political asylum 173, 174
Pollos Hermanos 206, 212, 213, 219, 223, 250
polyglot 257
portfolio 218
POW 161, 162
power 18, 43, 57, 69, 146, 154, 155, 159, 175, 179, 180, 184, 188, 198, 211,

221, 222, 227, 257, 259, 261
property 30, 43, 57, 61, 158, 160, 211, 214, 221
psychology 75, 100, 197, 247
psychopathy 203, 239
Ramallah 59, 67, 72, 83, 186
Revenge 219, 229
Revolutionary Guards 172, 173, 174
Rhea Seehorn 241
Romy Schneider 39
Rousseau 46, 143, 144, 145, 146, 209
Rupert Friend 169
Russia 61, 154, 157, 176, 183, 186, 187, 188, 193, 194
Sam Rockwell 29, 35
Saul Goodman 14, 202, 213, 237, 238, 244, 250, 254, 255, 256
Saul Goodman—Speedy justice for everyone! 237
Saulus 230, 232, 235, 255
Serge Gainsbourg 38
Sergei Mirov 157, 186, 187, 188, 194
Shin Bet 64, 69, 71, 74, 76, 80, 88, 94, 98, 105, 106, 109
Simone de Beauvoir 17, 38, 41, 50, 51, 52, 113
skateboard twins 241
slavery 21, 22, 24, 27
sovereignty 61, 62, 155, 181
stalemate 55, 106

state of nature 188, 210, 211
strength 43, 107, 154, 155, 159, 184, 188, 195, 198, 206, 209, 221, 222, 223, 224, 225
suicide 76, 89, 106, 141, 163, 165, 166, 171, 186, 187, 191, 254
suicide bombers 76
suicide vest 165, 166
Switzerland 61, 199
Syria 69, 77, 80, 100, 175
Taliban 178, 179, 180, 181, 182, 187, 188
Taraji P. Henson 29
Tel Aviv 66, 77, 90, 94, 95
Theodor Herzl 58, 70
Theodor W. Adorno 14, 18
Third World 141
Thomas Hobbes 7, 18, 143, 188, 197, 209, 210, 211, 220
Tit for tat 183
Todd Alquist 206
Tuco Salamanca 203, 241
Uncle Jack 207, 208, 224, 228, 229, 231, 234
US constitution 28, 32, 36, 156, 177, 254
US Delta Force 161
VHMET 114
violence 18, 21, 22, 23, 24, 29, 30, 43, 44, 65, 68, 79, 110, 143, 182, 198, 209, 221, 222, 223, 225, 234
virility 32

Voltaire 7, 14, 46, 143, 144, 237, 257, 258, 259, 260, 261, 262
Walt Whitman 216, 227
Walter White 18, 197, 198, 227, 230, 237, 245, 256
war crime 73
wardrobe malfunction 166
Woody Allen 210
Yevgeni Gromov 157, 176, 194

ibidem.eu